THE
Bible
Answer
BOOK

THE *Bible*
Answer
BOOK

R. A. Torrey

ɯ *Whitaker House*

Unless otherwise indicated, Scripture quotations are taken from the *New King James Version* (NKJV), © 1979, 1980, 1982 by Thomas Nelson, Inc. Used by permission. All rights reserved.

Scripture quotations marked (KJV) are taken from the *King James Version* of the Bible.

Scripture quotations marked (NAS) are from the *New American Standard Bible*, © 1960, 1962, 1968, 1971, 1973, 1975, 1977 by The Lockman Foundation. Used by permission.

Scripture quotations marked (NIV) are from the Holy Bible, *New International Version*, © 1973, 1978, 1984 by the International Bible Society. Used by permission.

Scripture quotations marked (RV) are taken from the *Revised Version* of the Holy Bible.

THE BIBLE ANSWER BOOK

ISBN: 0-88368-555-8
Printed in the United States of America
Copyright © 1999 by Whitaker House

Whitaker House
30 Hunt Valley Circle
New Kensington, PA 15068

Library of Congress Cataloging-in-Publication Data

Torrey, R. A. (Reuben Archer), 1856–1928.
    The Bible answer book / by R. A. Torrey.
       p.   cm.
    Includes index.
    ISBN 0-88368-555-8
    1. Bible—Miscellanea. 2. Christian life—Miscellanea. 3. Christian life—Biblical teaching. I. Title.
BS612.T635 1999
230'.041—dc21   99-19453

1 2 3 4 5 6 7 8 9 10 11 12 /09 08 07 06 05 04 03 02 01 00 99

CONTENTS

INTRODUCTION

Seasoned believers, new Christians, and those who are seeking God or exploring Christianity all have questions about the Bible and how to live the Christian life. In this book, renowned evangelist and Bible expert R. A. Torrey delves into some of the most perplexing questions people ask, such as "Why does God allow evil?"; "Is there an afterlife?"; "How can I get to heaven?"; "Why aren't all our prayers answered?"; "Who or what is the Antichrist?"; and "Are all religions the same?" He also provides practical advice for living the Christian life, addressing such issues as how to return to God if you've fallen away from Him, how to receive the Holy Spirit, how to have daily victory over sin, and how to study the Bible effectively.

This book is fascinating to read from cover to cover; it is also an extremely useful reference book to have on hand to answer questions that will come up as you grow in your faith and face new life situations.

Some topics are addressed in several different sections. In these instances, you will be referred to corresponding sections in the book. You may also find that some of the same material is covered in more than one question. This has been done to make each individual answer as complete as possible. In addition, Torrey includes biblical texts in many of his responses to give you a Scriptural basis for his answers and to enable you to do further study on

your own of these important topics. Additional
Scriptures have been included for further clarifica-
tion.

Reuben Archer Torrey is respected as one of the
greatest evangelists of modern times. Torrey was a
Congregational minister who joined Dwight L. Moody
in his evangelistic work in Chicago. Under Torrey's
direction, Moody Institute became a pattern for Bible
institutes around the world. At the turn of the twen-
tieth century, Torrey began his evangelistic tours and
campaigns, conducting a worldwide revival campaign
from 1903–05. He and his team ministered in many
parts of the world and reportedly brought nearly one
hundred thousand people to Jesus Christ. Torrey continued worldwide crusades for the next fifteen years,
reaching as far as Japan and China. During these
years, he also served as Dean of the Bible Institute of
Los Angeles and was pastor of the Church of the Open
Door in that city.

Torrey's straightforward style of evangelism has
led many people to Christ and has shown thousands
of Christians how to present the Gospel clearly and
effectively. In this book, you will discover how to address many important issues and challenges in your
Christian faith so that you may draw closer to Christ,
live a victorious Christian life, and be a credible wit-
ness to the Gospel.

THE BIBLE ANSWER BOOK

THE AFTERLIFE

Q: What becomes of our spirits when we die? Upon death, does one's soul pass directly to heaven or hell, or is there an intermediate state?

A: Immediately at death, the spirit of the believer departs to be with Christ in a state that is far better than the one in which it existed here on earth (Philippians 1:23). It is *"absent from the body and...at home with the Lord"* (2 Corinthians 5:8 NAS). But this is not the final state of blessedness of the redeemed. In our final state of blessedness, the spirit is not merely unclothed from its present mortal body but is clothed with its resurrection body. (See verses 1–4.) We will obtain this resurrection body at the second coming of Christ, when the bodies of those who sleep in Christ are raised from the dead and the bodies of believers then living are transformed in the twinkling of an eye—when our perishable bodies become imperishable. (See 1 Thessalonians 4:15–17; 1 Corinthians 15:51–53.)

On the other hand, immediately at death, the spirits of the wicked depart into that portion of hades reserved for the wicked dead, where they consciously exist in great torment. (See Luke 16:19–31.) But this is not their final condition of torment. At the close of the Millennium—the thousand-year reign of Christ on earth after His second coming—those who have died in sin will be raised again to stand before the Great White Throne of God, to be judged and assigned to their final condition of torment. (See Revelation 20:11–15; 21:8.) It is then that they will enter into their final and fullest suffering. Just as the redeemed spirits will be clothed at the coming of Christ with their glorious resurrection bodies, which will be perfect counterparts of the redeemed spirits that inhabit them and partakers with them in all their joy, the wicked are to be clothed with bodies that will be perfect counterparts of the lost spirits that inhabit them and will be partakers with them in all their misery.

ALCOHOL

Q: Should a Christian drink alcohol, or should he abstain from it?

A: One of the most common and destructive sins of our time is that of excessive drinking. I urge upon Christians total abstinence for their own sake and for the sake of others. I make it a point that if a person can do just as well without intoxicating beverages, then he ought to do without them for the sake of his brother (see 1 Corinthians 8:4–13). However, if he cannot do just as well without them, then he ought to do without them for his own sake.

Q: What should a person do whose spouse continually drinks?

A: If your spouse continually drinks, you should first go to God in prayer. God will reveal to you if there is anything in you that causes your spouse to drink. If you are angry and totally disagreeable in the home, while in a prayer meeting seem totally sweet and angelic, you should first get thoroughly right with God and then filled with the Holy Spirit. In this way, you may show, through the Spirit-filled life, the beauty of holiness. Your spouse will be attracted and won by this. Then pray and watch for an opportunity to speak to your spouse—to move heaven and earth and never quit until your spouse is converted.

ANNIHILATION OF THE WICKED

Q: What is meant by the theory of the annihilation of the wicked?

A: It means the annihilation of the existence of those who die without having accepted Jesus Christ as their Savior.

Q: Why is the theory of the annihilation of the wicked, supposedly indicated by Revelation 20:14–15, unscriptural and a reprehensible doctrine?

A: The annihilation of the wicked is not indicated in Revelation 20:14–15 to anyone who reads the whole passage and parallel passages in the Scriptures. The passage reads: *"Then Death and Hades were cast into the lake of fire. This is the second death. And anyone not found written in the Book of Life was cast into the lake of fire."* The fate of those cast into the lake of fire is not annihilation. There is no Scripture to support such a theory. The Bible clearly teaches that the future destiny of the wicked is a condition of unresting, unending, conscious torment and anguish. (Please refer to the section "Eternal Punishment" in this book.)

As to its being a "reprehensible doctrine," I would say that I have never known anyone who accepted this doctrine who did not lose power in serving God. I could give examples of men whom God greatly used who have been led to accept this doctrine and who, in consequence, have been in part or altogether set aside as soulwinners. If one really believes the doctrine of the endless, conscious torment of the unrepentant, he will work as never before for their salvation before it is too late.

THE ANTICHRIST

Q: Who is the Antichrist, and when will he appear?

A: The Antichrist will be a person in whom Satan's resistance to Christ and His kingdom will culminate. He will be a man, but a man whom Satan will fill to such an extent that he will be Satan incarnate. The Devil always seeks to mimic God's work, and his mimicking of God's work will culminate in his mimicking of the incarnation of God in Jesus Christ. The Antichrist's coming will be *"according to the working of Satan, with all power, signs, and lying wonders, and with all unrighteous deception"* (2 Thessalonians 2:9–10).

The Antichrist will appear just prior to the second coming of Jesus Christ, and our Lord will *"consume* [him] *with the breath of His mouth and destroy* [him] *with the brightness of His coming"* (v. 8).

There are already many antichrists preparing the way for the final and consummate Antichrist (1 John 2:18). Indeed, everyone who denies the Father and the Son is an antichrist (v. 22), but there seems to be a special preparation for *the* Antichrist, in whom all the forces of evil will coalesce. These forces of evil will join and be headed by one man whom the Devil will especially gift and in whom he will dwell, and that man will be the Antichrist.

ASSURANCE OF SALVATION

Q: Is it right for a person to say that he is saved? In other words, may I know that I am saved, and if so, on what authority?

A: If you really are saved, you may know it on the authority of God's Word. God says in John 3:36, *"He who believes in the Son **has** everlasting life"* (emphasis added). You know whether you believe in the Son or not. If you do believe in the Son, you know you have everlasting life because God says so here in so many words.

This is also emphasized in 1 John 5:11–12: *"And this is the testimony: that God has given us eternal life, and this life is in His Son. He who has the Son has life; he who does not have the Son of God does not have life."* When one who believes in the Son doubts that he has life, he makes God a liar. This is indicated in the preceding verse, where we read: *"He who does not believe God has made Him a liar, because he has not believed the testimony that God has given of His Son"* (v. 10).

Furthermore, anyone who has received Jesus as his Savior and Lord and King may know that he is a child of God. God says so in so many words in John 1:12: *"But as many as received Him, to them He gave the right to become children of God."* If you have received Jesus, you have a right to call yourself a child of God. You have no right to doubt that you are a child of God.

Again, everyone who believes in Jesus has a right to know that he is justified, that his sins are all forgiven, and that God regards him as righteous in Christ. He has a right to know it on the very best authority, namely, because God says so. We read in Acts 13:38–39: *"Therefore let it be known to you, brethren, that through this Man is preached to you the forgiveness of sins; and by Him everyone who believes is justified from all things."* Notice that it says, *"Everyone who believes is justified."* You know whether you believe or not. If you do believe in Jesus, God says you are justified. Many people doubt their salvation because they rely on their feelings instead of looking at the Word of God. It is not at all a question of whether you *feel* that you are a child of God; it is simply a question of what God says. If you rely on your feelings instead of the Word of God, you make God a liar for the sake of your own feelings.

God caused the book of 1 John to be written for the very purpose that everyone who believes in the Son of God might know that he has eternal life: *"These things [are] written to you who believe in the name of the Son of God, that you may **know** that you have eternal life"* (1 John 5:13, emphasis added). If God caused a book of the Bible to be written so that we might know this, then certainly we may know it. The above verse teaches us that the way to know it is from what is *"written."* The first thing to be sure of is that you really do believe in Jesus—that you really have received Him as your Savior, surrendered to Him as your Lord and Master, and confessed Him as such publicly. When you are sure of this, you may be absolutely sure that you are saved, that you have eternal life, that your sins are totally forgiven, and that you are a child of God.

THE ATONEMENT

Q: What theory of atonement does the Bible teach?

A: The Bible does not teach a theory of atonement. It teaches a fact, the glorious fact that every one of our sins was laid upon Jesus Christ. (See Isaiah 53:6; 2 Corinthians 5:21; Galatians 3:13; 1 Peter 2:24.) As a result of Jesus Christ having borne our sins, there is not only pardon for every sin but also justification, which is more than pardon. The Bible teaches that because Jesus Christ took our place on the cross, the moment we accept Jesus Christ, we step into His place, the place of perfect acceptance before God. We become *"the righteousness of God in Him"* (2 Corinthians 5:21). We no longer have our own poor, pitiable, unsatisfactory righteousness but a perfect righteousness, the righteousness of God in Christ (Philippians 3:9).

Q: How could God punish His innocent Son for the guilt of man?

A: The doctrine of the Bible is not that God, a holy first person, takes the sins of man, a guilty second person, and lays them upon His own holy Son, an innocent third person. That is the way the doctrine is often misrepresented. In fact, it is the depiction usually made by those who reject the Bible doctrine of substitution—that Christ, as our Substitute, suffered and died for our sins in our place.

The real teaching of the Bible is that Jesus Christ is not a third person, but that He is indeed the first person—*"that God was in Christ reconciling the world to Himself"* (2 Corinthians 5:19). In the atoning death of His Son, instead of laying the punishment of guilty man upon an innocent third person, God took the shame and suffering due to man upon Himself. That is the complete opposite of being unjust and cruel—it is amazing grace!

Furthermore, Jesus Christ was also the second person. He was not merely *a* man, He was the Son of Man, the representative Man, the Head of the race. No ordinary man could bear the guilt of other men, but the Son of Man, the representative Man, could.

If we take the teaching of the Bible as a complete whole and not in a fragmentary way, it is the most wonderful philosophy the world has ever known. We will ponder and admire its inexhaustible depths throughout eternity. But if we take any one doctrine out of the Bible, the other doctrines become absurd. If we give up the doctrine of the deity of Jesus Christ, then the doctrine of the Atonement becomes an absurdity, and the difficulty suggested by this question naturally arises. Or if we give up the doctrine of the real humanity of Christ, the doctrine of the Atonement loses its profound significance. But if we take all that the Bible says, namely, that Jesus was really divine, *"God...manifested in the flesh"* (1 Timothy 3:16), and that He was truly man, not merely *a* man but the Son of Man, the representative Man, then the doctrine of the Atonement does not present any difficulties. Rather, it presents an amazing depth of truth.

It is strange how little the average objector to the doctrine of substitution knows about the real doctrine of the Bible on this point. Instead of fighting what the Bible really teaches, he is fighting a figment of his own uninstructed imagination.

BACKSLIDING

Q: How would you deal with a backslider? Is there hope for him, and how?

A: Everywhere I go, I find many people who tell me that they were once Christians, but who confess that they have gone back into the world. I am persuaded that many of these people were never truly saved. They have gone forward in revival meetings, have joined the church, or have done something of that sort, but they have never really fully accepted Jesus Christ as their Savior and Lord. Having failed in their first attempt, they hesitate to make another.

This hesitation is unreasonable. The fact that one has attempted to do something and has done it in the wrong way is no reason for not doing it in the right way. If people would begin the Christian life correctly, they would not be so likely to go back into the world. Also, if they have begun it in the wrong way, they had better begin it over again in the right way. As God's own Word shows us, this is the right way to begin:

♦ First, accept Jesus Christ as Savior. That is, believe God's testimony concerning Him— that He bore all your sins in His own body on the cross—and trust God to forgive you, not because of anything that you have done but because of what Christ did when He made full atonement for your sins. (See 1 Peter 2:24; Galatians 3:13.)

♦ Second, accept Jesus Christ as your Lord and King (Acts 2:36). This involves the utter surrender of your mind to Him, so that it may be renewed by Him, and of your life to Him, so that it may be governed by Him. You must put yourself completely at His disposal. You

21

must not only sing "I surrender all" with your lips, but you must also make it a fact in your life. This lack of absolute surrender at the time of starting the Christian life is the cause of a large measure of backsliding.

♦ Third, accept Christ as the risen Son of God who has all power in heaven and on earth (Matthew 28:18), and trust Him day by day to keep you from falling and from all the power of sin and temptation. (See Hebrews 7:25; Jude 24.)

When you have begun right, most of the battle is won, but you must continue in obedience to Christ. Continuance in the Christian life is not at all a question of your strength, but of Christ's. If you have begun the Christian life once and failed, begin it again and succeed. Many of the strongest Christians today are those who were once backsliders. The apostle Peter himself was once a backslider, but after Pentecost, he was one of the mightiest servants of Christ that the world ever saw. Pentecost is possible for you.

No one can be more miserable than the backslider. Jeremiah was certainly right when he said to backsliding Israel, *"It is an evil and bitter thing that you have forsaken the LORD your God"* (Jeremiah 2:19). The one who forsakes Christ forsakes the *"fountain of living waters, and* [digs himself] *cisterns; broken cisterns that can hold no water"* (v. 13). Let him leave the broken cisterns of the world and come back to Christ, the Fountain of Living Water.

BAPTISM

Q: Is baptism necessary for salvation?

A: It depends upon what you mean by the words *salvation* and *baptism*. Certainly, some have found forgiveness of sins and have entered into eternal life without water baptism, such as the thief on the cross. (See Luke 23:39–43.) There is a body of believers who do not practice water baptism at all, namely the Friends, who are also called Quakers. Many of the Friends have the consciousness of having their sins forgiven, and God has set His seal upon their acceptance by giving them the gift of the Holy Spirit.

However, the term *salvation* is used in Scripture not merely in regard to forgiveness of sins and eternal life, but also in a larger sense of all the fullness of blessing that is to be found in Christ. Certainly, one cannot enter into all the fullness of blessing that there is in Christ without absolute obedience to Him (Acts 5:32). If there is any commandment of Christ that we know we do not obey, we certainly cannot enjoy fullness of fellowship with Him. Jesus Christ Himself commanded water baptism (Matthew 28:19). He also commanded it through His disciples (Acts 2:38). As an act of obedience to Christ, therefore, water baptism certainly is, in the larger sense, a saving ordinance for those who believe that Jesus Christ commands it. Submitting to baptism has been the turning point in the experience of many men and women. It has been done as an act of conscious obedience to Jesus Christ, and has been accompanied by great blessing.

There are earnest followers of Christ who do not see in such passages as the above a command to baptize or be baptized with water, and in not being baptized, they are not consciously disobeying Jesus Christ. It is difficult for me to see how anyone can study the New Testament with the single-minded purpose of discovering what it actually teaches and not see the necessity of water baptism. Yet from my contact with those believers known as Friends, I must conclude that many of them are perfectly conscientious Christians, even though they have not been baptized with water, and that they are true children of God.

Q: What is the explanation of 1 Corinthians 15:29: *"What will they do who are baptized for the dead, if the dead do not rise at all? Why then are they baptized for the dead?"*

A: In Paul's time, there seems to have been a custom in which people were baptized on behalf of those who, for one reason or another, had died without baptism. The above verse is the only reference in Scripture to this custom. It evidently was not a custom that the Bible commanded or sanctioned. Paul was not sanctioning it here. He simply referred to it as existing, and he referred to those who practiced it as showing that they believed in the resurrection, for otherwise this baptism for the dead would have no significance.

The custom of baptism for the dead was practiced for a time, but only among heretics. It was repudiated by the church. Many customs crept into the church very early on that were not of God, that the apostles did not endorse, and that ought not to be followed by us. The Mormons practice the custom today, and this verse, which they use as a warrant for it, does not support the custom. Certainly, if Paul had wanted us to follow this custom, he would have said something more about it than he did in this Scripture verse. He would at least have endorsed it, and he did not. When we look at the verse carefully, we see that Paul not only did not endorse it but also by implication rejected it, for he separated himself from the custom by saying, *"What will **they** do who are baptized for the dead?"* By this word *"they,"* he not only separated himself from it but also separated those to whom he wrote from this third party who were baptized for the dead.

THE BIBLE

Q: Do you believe in the verbal inspiration of the Bible?

A: I do. That is, I believe that the writers of the various books of the Bible were guided by the Holy Spirit, not only in the thoughts to which they gave expression but also in the choice of the words in which they expressed the thoughts. They *"spoke from God as they were carried along by the Holy Spirit"* (2 Peter 1:21 NIV). It was the Holy Spirit who spoke. The words that were uttered were His words. (See 2 Samuel 23:2; Hebrews 3:7–8; 10:15–16; Acts 28:25.) The very words that were used were the words that the Holy Spirit taught. Nothing could be plainer than Paul's statement: *"These things we also speak, not in words which man's wisdom teaches but which the Holy Spirit teaches"* (1 Corinthians 2:13).

The Holy Spirit Himself anticipated all these modern, ingenious but unbiblical and false theories regarding His own work in the apostles. The more carefully and minutely one studies the wording of the statements made in the Bible, the more he will become convinced of the marvelous accuracy of the words that were used to produce the thoughts. To a superficial student, the doctrine of verbal inspiration may appear questionable or even absurd, but any regenerated and Spirit-taught person who ponders the words of Scripture day after day and year after year will become increasingly convinced that the wisdom of God is in the very words used as well as in the thoughts that are expressed in the words.

It is a very significant fact that our difficulties with the Bible rapidly disappear when we come to notice the precise language that is used. The change of a word or a letter, of a tense, case, or number, often lands a person in contradiction or untruth. However, by taking the words just as they were written, difficulties disappear, and the truth shines forth. The more microscopically we study the Bible, the more clearly its divine origin shines forth as we see its perfection of form as well as of substance.

Q: Are all parts of the Bible equally inspired by God?

A: *"All Scripture is given by inspiration of God* [is God-breathed]*"* (2 Timothy 3:16, emphasis added). There is no warrant for the change that the Revised Version makes in this passage: *"Every scripture inspired of God...."* As originally written, the entire Bible was infallible truth, and in our English versions, we have the original writings translated with substantial accuracy. But not all parts of the Bible are equally important. For example, the genealogies given in the first nine chapters of 1 Chronicles are important, far more important than the average student of the Bible realizes, but they certainly are not as important to the believer today as the teachings of Christ and the apostles.

Q: If the Holy Spirit is the author of the words of Scripture, how do we account for variations in style and wording? For example, how do we account for the fact that Paul always uses Pauline language, and John Johannine language, and so on?

A: Even if we could not account at all for this fact, it would have little weight against the explicit statements of God's Word. Anyone who is humble enough and wise enough to recognize that there are a great many things that we cannot account for at all that could be easily accounted for if we knew a little more, is never staggered by an apparent difficulty of this kind. But in point of fact, it is easy enough to account for these variations. The simple explanation is this: the Holy Spirit is wise enough and has facility enough in the use of language in revealing truth, to and through any individual, to use words, phrases, and forms of expression that are in that person's vocabulary and forms of thought to which that person is accustomed, and in every way to make use of that person's particular individuality. It is one of the many signs of the divine wisdom of this Book that the same divine truth is expressed with absolute accuracy in such widely varying forms of expression.

Q: If the Bible is verbally inspired, why did the gospel writers not give Jesus' and other people's words exactly? I can understand how their accounts of events may differ, but Jesus' words cannot properly be rendered one way by Matthew and another way by Luke if verbal inspiration is correct. Note that Galatians 3:16 stresses the importance of accurate wording in Scripture: *"Now to Abraham and his Seed were the promises made. He does not say, 'And to seeds,' as of many, but as of one, 'And to your Seed,' who is Christ.*

A: The gospel writers did give people's words exactly when they claimed to give them exactly. When they only claimed to give the substance of what people said, the words may not be given exactly as they were spoken. But even when the gospel writers gave Jesus' words exactly, they did not always claim to record everything that He said, so that the book of Matthew may give part of what He said, and Luke another part of what He said. To get all that He said, both accounts must be taken together. Matthew gave the part that was adapted to the purpose of his book, and Luke gave the part that was adapted to his. It is well that they were given in just this way, for it is one of the many incidental proofs that the Gospels are independent of one another and were not composed by writers who were in collusion with one another.

Furthermore, it must be kept in mind that the words of Jesus recorded by Matthew and Luke were spoken in Aramaic and were translated by Matthew and Luke into Greek. There is reason to suppose that the utterances recorded by Matthew, Mark, and Luke were largely utterances that Jesus gave in Aramaic, while those recorded by John were largely those that Jesus spoke in Greek. It must be remembered that in the time of Jesus, the people in Palestine were a bilingual people.

Q: How would you endeavor to interest an indifferent person in the study of the Bible?

A: First of all, I would have to get him to accept Jesus Christ as his Savior. Then I would show him that the Bible is God's Word to him and that the only way to be strong and to grow in grace is to study the Word. I would then explain to him some simple method of Bible study and have him begin doing it. The best way for a converted person to become interested in the study of the Bible is to actually start studying it. The more one studies it, the more his taste for Bible study increases.

Q: What books of the Bible should a young convert read or study first?

A: First of all, he should read the gospel of John. It is one of the most profound books of the Bible, and yet there is much in it for the youngest believer. It was written for the specific purpose of bringing people to believe that *"Jesus is the Christ, the Son of God, and that believing* [they might] *have life in His name"* (John 20:31). There is nothing that the young believer needs more than to come to an intelligent, fixed faith in Jesus as the Christ, the Son of God.

After the gospel of John, I would have the young disciple read the gospel of Mark, then Luke, then Matthew. After that, I would urge him to study the Acts of the Apostles and then the epistle to the Romans. I think that, after that, I would have him read through the whole New Testament starting from the beginning.

Q: There are some verses in the Bible that are not translated in the way you know they were intended to be. When a person takes up those points with you, what do you tell him?

A: I tell him that we know now what the correct translation is, and I show him what it is. Not one fundamental doctrine has been affected by the variations in manuscripts or in translations.

THE CHRISTIAN LIFE

Q: What advice do you give for having a consistent and abundant Christian life?

A: The Bible gives us seven steps to an abundant Christian life:

♦ First, begin right. John 1:12 tells us what a right beginning is: *"But as many as received Him, to them He gave the right to become children of God, to those who believe in His name."* Receive Christ as your Savior who died for your sin. Trust the whole matter of your forgiveness to Him. Rest upon the fact that He has paid the full penalty for your sin. *"For He made Him who knew no sin to be sin for us, that we might become the righteousness of God in Him"* (2 Corinthians 5:21). Take Him as your Deliverer who will save you from the power of sin, who will give life to those who are dead in trespasses and sins. Don't try to save yourself from the power of sin; trust Him to do it. Take Him as your Master. Don't seek to guide your own life. Surrender unconditionally to His lordship over you. The life of entire surrender is a joyous life all along the way. If you have never before received Christ as your Savior and surrendered your life to Him, and if you wish to make a success of the Christian life, get alone with God and say, "All for Jesus."

♦ Second, confess Christ openly before men. *"Therefore whoever confesses Me before men, him I will also confess before My Father who is in heaven"* (Matthew 10:32). *"For with the heart one believes unto righteousness, and with the mouth confession is made unto salvation"* (Romans 10:10). The life of confession is the life of full salvation.

♦ Third, study the Word. *"As newborn babes, desire the pure milk of the word, that you may grow thereby"* (1 Peter 2:2). The Word of God is the soul's food. It is the nourishment of the new life. A person who neglects the Word

32

cannot make much of a success of the Christian life. All who do well in the Christian life are great feeders on the Word of God.

♦ Fourth, *"pray without ceasing"* (1 Thessalonians 5:17). The one who wants to succeed in the Christian life must lead a life of prayer. This is easy enough if you just begin to do it.

Have set times for prayer. The rule of David and Daniel, three times a day, is a good rule. David wrote, *"Evening and morning and at noon I will pray, and cry aloud, and He shall hear my voice"* (Psalm 55:17). The book of Daniel records, *"Now when Daniel knew that the writing was signed* [which decreed that no one could pray to any god or man except the king of Persia], *he went home. And in his upper room, with his windows open toward Jerusalem, he knelt down on his knees three times that day, and prayed and gave thanks before his God, as was his custom since early days"* (Daniel 6:10). Begin the day with thanksgiving and prayer—thanksgiving for the definite mercies of the past, and prayer for the definite needs of the present day. Stop in the midst of the bustle and worry and temptation of the day for thanksgiving and prayer. Close the day with thanksgiving and prayer.

Then there should be special prayer in special temptation—when we see the temptation approaching. Keep looking to God. It is not necessary that we be on our knees all the time.

However, the *heart* should be on its knees all the time.

There are three things for which the person who wants to make a success of the Christian life must especially pray. First, he must pray for wisdom: *"If any of you lacks wisdom, let him ask of God"* (James 1:5). Second, he must pray for strength: *"Those who wait on the LORD shall renew their strength"* (Isaiah 40:31). Third, he must pray for the Holy Spirit: *"Your heavenly Father* [will] *give the Holy Spirit to those who ask Him"* (Luke 11:13). If you have not yet received the baptism with the Holy Spirit, you should offer definite prayer for this definite blessing and definitely expect to receive it. If you have already received the baptism with the Holy Spirit, you should, with each new emergency that you encounter in your Christian life and ministry, pray to God for a new filling with the Holy Spirit. (See Acts 4:18–31.)

♦ Fifth, go to work for Christ. *"For to everyone who has, more will be given, and he will have abundance; but from him who does not have, even what he has will be taken away"* (Matthew 25:29). The context of this verse is that those who use what they have will get more, and those who let what they have lie idle will lose even that. The working Christian—the one who uses his talents, whether few or many, in Christ's service—is the one who does well in the Christian life here, and who will hereafter hear, *"Well done, good and faithful servant; you were faithful over a few things, I will make you ruler over many things. Enter into the joy of your lord"* (v. 21). Find some work to do for Christ, and do it. Look for work. If it is nothing more than distributing tracts, do it. Always be looking for something more to do for Christ, and you will always be receiving something more from Christ.

♦ Sixth, give generously. *"The generous soul will be made rich"* (Proverbs 11:25). *"He who sows sparingly will also reap sparingly, and he who sows bountifully will also reap bountifully....And God is able to make all grace abound toward you, that you, always having all sufficiency in all things, may have an abundance for every good work"* (2 Corinthians 9:6, 8). Success and growth in the Christian life depend on few things more than on generous giving. A stingy Christian cannot be a growing Christian. It is wonderful how a Christian begins to grow when he begins to give.

♦ Seventh, keep pushing on. *"Brothers, I do not consider myself yet to have taken hold of it. But one thing I do: forgetting what is behind and straining toward what is ahead, I press on toward the goal to win the prize for which God has called me heavenward in Christ Jesus"* (Philippians 3:13–14 NIV).

Forget the sins that lie behind you. If you fail anywhere, if you fall, don't be discouraged, don't give up, don't brood over the sin. Confess it instantly. Believe God's Word: *"If we confess our sins, He is faithful and just to forgive us our sins and to cleanse us from all unrighteousness"* (1 John 1:9). Believe that the sin is forgiven, forget it, and press on. Satan deceives many of us in regard to this. He keeps us brooding over our failures and sins.

In addition, forget the achievements and victories of the past, and press on to greater ones. Here, too, Satan cheats many of us out of the abundant life. He keeps us thinking so much about what we have already obtained, and he makes us so contented with it and so puffed up over it, that we come to a standstill or even backslide. Our only safety is in forgetting the things that are behind and pressing on. There is always something better ahead, until we *"come...to a perfect man, to the measure of the stature of the fullness of Christ"* (Ephesians 4:13).

CHRISTIAN SCIENCE

Q: How would you prove the error of Christian Science?

A: Many are being led astray into Christian Science. Most Christian Scientists claim to believe the Bible. Take them, therefore, to 1 John 4:1–3: *"Beloved, do not believe every spirit, but test the spirits, whether they are of God; because many false prophets have gone out into the world. By this you know the Spirit of God: every spirit that confesses that Jesus Christ has come in the flesh is of God, and every spirit that does not confess that Jesus Christ has come in the flesh is not of God. And this is the spirit of the Antichrist, which you have heard was coming, and is now already in the world."*

This passage strikes at the very foundation of Christian Science. As one of its fundamental doctrines, Christian Science denies the reality of matter, the reality of the body, and (of necessity) the reality of the Incarnation. Show them by this passage that the Bible says that every spirit that does not confess that Jesus Christ came in the flesh is not of God, but of antichrist, and therefore any doctrine that denies the Incarnation is not Christian.

Q: Why do you believe that Christian Science founder Mary Baker Eddy's claim that she received the tenets of Christian Science by divine inspiration is false?

A: First of all, I know that her claim is false because it has been proven that she got her theories from a man by whom she was treated.* When she wrote her first book in its original form, she did not claim that it was her original work or that she had received it from God; she truly acknowledged that she was writing down the views of this person by whom she had been treated and under whom she had studied.

In the second place, I know that her claim is false because the tenets themselves are false. Mrs. Eddy denies the reality of the Incarnation, and this is one of the primary tests of the truth or falsehood of any system or doctrine. This is the decisive question to ask of any spirit and any system of doctrines, as shown in the previous answer. Mrs. Eddy also denies the Atonement, the fundamental truth of the Gospel. Her view of the Atonement is not the one taught in the Bible, namely, that Jesus Christ Himself bore our sins in His own body on the cross. (See 2 Corinthians 5:21; Galatians 3:13; 1 Peter 2:24.) These are only some of the many great errors in the teaching of Mrs. Eddy.

There are, it is true, some elements of truth in the teachings of Christian Science. Every false system must have some true teachings in it; otherwise, it could not have any success at all. Every dangerous system of error takes some truth and distorts and perverts it and covers it up with a large amount of error. That the mind has a tremendous influence

---

*Phineas Parkhurst Quimby, a well-known and influential mental healer. *Editor's note.*

over the body and that much disease can be overcome through the mind is unquestionably true. That God answers prayer and, in answer to prayer, heals the sick, is taught in the Bible and taught by experience. That Jesus Christ had a mission for the body as well as for the soul is clearly taught in Scripture. That a great deal of harm has been done by the use of drugs, every wise physician admits. Mrs. Eddy has taken these truths, which the church has often lost sight of, and has opened the door for the introduction of a vast amount of destructive and damning error. If the church had been truer to its own mission and had given people a real and full and satisfying Gospel, the great majority of those who have fallen prey to Mrs. Eddy's teaching would have escaped the snare.

THE CHURCH

Q: What are the conditions of entrance into the church?

A: The word *church* in the New Testament is used, first, of the whole body of believers in Jesus Christ. (See Matthew 16:18; Acts 2:47; 20:28; Ephesians 5:24–25; Colossians 1:18, 24.) Second, it is used of the body of believers in any one place—for example, the church of the Thessalonians (1 Thessalonians 1:1). Third, it is used of the local congregations meeting regularly for worship, teaching, and the breaking of bread— for example, the church that met in Rome in the home of Priscilla and Aquila (Romans 16:3–5).

The conditions of entrance into the church in its first and deepest meaning are acceptance of Jesus Christ as one's personal Savior, surrender to Him as Lord and Master, and open confession of Him before the world (Romans 10:9–10). The conditions of entrance into local churches are determined by the churches themselves. Most churches receive members upon satisfactory evidence that they have really forsaken sin, accepted Christ as their personal Savior, and surrendered their lives to Him. Some churches require subscription to a creed, more or less detailed. For example, it might include general affirmations of faith or also more detailed beliefs of the church's denomination. Some evangelical denominations require water baptism on the part of the applicant for membership. (See Acts 2:38, 41, 47.)

Q: What does Matthew 16:18 mean: *"You are Peter, and on this rock I will build My church"*? Does this verse teach that Peter was the rock upon which Christ would build His church, and does it prove that the Roman Catholic Church, as built upon Peter, is the only true church?

A: The passage does not teach that Peter was the rock upon which Christ would build His church.

Peter's name in Greek is *Petros,* meaning "a piece of rock." The word translated *"rock"* in the above verse is *petra,* which means "a rock." Peter had just made a confession of Jesus as *"the Christ, the Son of the living God"* (v. 16). Jesus, as the Christ, the Son of the living God, is the Rock upon which the church is built. *"No other foundation can anyone lay than that which is laid, which is Jesus Christ"* (1 Corinthians 3:11). Peter, by his faith in Jesus as the Christ, the Son of God, and by his confession of Him as such, became a piece of the Rock. Every believer, by believing in Jesus as the Christ, the Son of the living God, and by confessing Him as such, becomes a piece of the Rock and, in this sense, a part of the foundation upon which the church is built, *"Jesus Christ Himself being the chief corner stone"* (Ephesians 2:20; see also verses 21–22).

Furthermore, the Roman Catholic Church is not built upon Peter. There is no real evidence that Peter was the first bishop of the church of Rome. Even if he were, that would not prove that those who followed him in the office were his true successors. The true successors of Peter are those who build on the same Christ that Peter built upon, who teach the same doctrine, and who exhibit the same life.

Q: Was Peter the first pope?

A: No, he was not. There was no pope until long after Peter was dead and buried. The papacy was a later outgrowth of the church of which there was not even an apparent seed in the days of Peter. Peter was far from being a pope. Consider the fact that the apostle Paul rebuked him openly (Galatians 2:11–14).

As I explained in the previous answer, there is no proof that Peter was ever bishop of the church in Rome; there is no decisive proof that he was ever in Rome. However, even if he was, he certainly was not a pope in any sense that the word now carries. There is nothing in the Bible that warrants such an office as that of pope. In fact, Jesus Christ expressly forbids any man from holding such an office. He said in Matthew 23:8–10, *"Do not be called 'Rabbi'; for One is your Teacher, the Christ, and you are all brethren. Do not call anyone on earth your father; for One is your Father, He who is in heaven. And do not be called teachers; for One is your Teacher, the Christ."* Now, the pope claims to be a "father" in the very sense used here, in the very sense that Jesus forbids any man to be called father.

Q: What does Matthew 16:19 mean: *"I will give you the keys of the kingdom of heaven, and whatever you bind on earth will be bound in heaven, and whatever you loose on earth will be loosed in heaven"*? Does this teach that Peter had the power to admit anyone to the kingdom of heaven or shut him out, and that therefore the Roman Catholic Church, built upon Peter, is the true church?

A: No, it does not teach anything of the kind. When anyone studied under a Jewish rabbi, it was the custom of the rabbi to give him a key when he had become perfect in the doctrine, signifying that he was now able to unlock the secrets of the kingdom. Christ's words refer to this custom. Peter, by his confession of Jesus as the Christ, the Son of God, had proven that the Father was revealing the truth to him (v. 17), and Jesus looked forward to the day when, filled with the Holy Spirit, Peter would be guided into all the truth (John 16:12–14) and thus be competent to unlock the kingdom to men. Every Spirit-filled person, everyone taught by the Holy Spirit, has the keys of the kingdom of heaven. He has spiritual discernment and is competent to unlock the kingdom to men.

"Binding" and "loosing" were common expressions in Jesus' day for forbidding and permitting. What a rabbi forbade, he was said to "bind." What he permitted, he was said to "loose." Peter and the other disciples, as Spirit-filled men, would have discernment to know what God permitted and what God forbade. Whatever Peter, as a Spirit-filled man, forbade on earth would be forbidden in heaven, and whatever he permitted would be permitted in heaven.

We see Peter, on the Day of Pentecost, using the keys to unlock the kingdom to the Jews, and three thousand people entered into the kingdom that day. In Acts 10, we see Peter now using the keys to unlock the kingdom to the Gentiles, and a whole household entered into the kingdom that day.

Every time anyone preaches the Gospel in the power of the Holy Spirit, he is using the keys. Not only did Peter have the keys, but we may have them today. Since we are taught by the Spirit, we may have discernment as to what God permits and what God forbids. Then, what we forbid here on earth will be the thing that God forbids in heaven and what we permit will be the thing that God permits in heaven.

Q: What should an earnest Christian do in a day when the churches are so full of worldliness and error as they are today? Should he join the church?

A: Yes. I fully recognize the worldliness that is in many churches today and the error that is taught from many pulpits. But after all is said, the church is the best organization there is in the world. What would the world be today if it were not for the churches that are in it? The churches, even with all their present imperfections, are the institutions that are saving society from utter corruption.

Any Christian can accomplish more for the salvation of souls and the upbuilding of Christian character and the good of the community by uniting with some church than he can by trying to live a Christian life all by himself. There may be times when a person has to voice his protest against sins of a glaring nature in some individual church, and, if his protest will not be heard, it may be necessary for him to withdraw as a testimony against that church. But these occasions are comparatively rare.

Great corruption—unspeakable immorality, in fact—had crept into the church in Corinth, and yet Paul did not hint for a moment to any of the members of that church that they should withdraw from it. He did write to them that they should judge the person who had committed sexual immorality with his own father's wife, and to put him out of the church, but he never suggested that they should withdraw from the church. (See 1 Corinthians 5:1–13.) Even Jesus did not withdraw from the synagogues of His day until He was put out of them. (See Luke 4:15–30.) Synagogue worship had become full of formality and error, and yet it was the custom of our Lord to attend the synagogue on the Sabbath day (v. 16). The apostle Paul followed His example in this matter (Acts 17:2). There are many earnest Christian men and women today who have lost all power and influence for God and good in the community by abandoning their fellowship with other believers who were not as well instructed as they, and by giving themselves up to harsh and condemning criticism.

Some Christians justify their actions by saying that the book of Revelation tells us to "come out of Babylon." (See Revelation 18:1–4.) The word *Babylon* is used in this context to symbolize the spirit of immorality and idolatry that will culminate in the Antichrist. While it is true that the Bible says to "come out of Babylon," Babylon, in this ultimate sense, has not yet been formed. Everything in the book of Revelation after the first verse of the fourth chapter describes the time after the Rapture of the church, not the present time. To apply this command to "come out of Babylon" to the present time and the present state of the churches is to handle the Word of God deceitfully and not rightly divide the Word of Truth (2 Timothy 2:15).

Of course, if the pastor of a church persistently preaches glaring and pernicious error, one should protest against it and should not allow his children to sit under that kind of false doctrine. But again, these occasions are comparatively rare.

Q: Do you believe in having different denominations? Do sects do more harm than good in the cause of religion?

A: Undoubtedly, sects do more harm than good in the cause of religion, for the very idea of a sect is of something that causes division. The animating spirit of the sect is division.

However, a denomination is not necessarily a sect. The different denominations have arisen because different people saw some truths very clearly that others did not see, and around these people other people have gathered to enforce that particular aspect of truth. For example, the Congregationalists and the Presbyterians arose in England and Scotland to stand for the truth of the liberty of the individual believer. Many other truths were associated with this truth in the development of these denominations. The Quakers arose to stand for the truth of the illumination and guidance of the Holy Spirit for the individual believer today. The Methodists arose to stand for the truth of a definite personal experience of regeneration and the necessity of a holy life. Afterward, other truths, such as the freedom of the will, became prominently associated with these truths in the teaching of the Methodist denomination. By standing strongly for some neglected truths that needed to be emphasized, the denominations have undoubtedly done good. In the present imperfect state of man, where no individual is large enough to take in the whole scope of God's truth, and where one man sees one line of truth strongly and another man another line of truth, denominations have been necessary. But it is fitting that denominational lines are now less defined and that each denomination is coming to understand and accept the truths for which other denominations have stood.

Q: What do you think of the institutional church? Is it not detrimental to the real work of the church as set forth in the New Testament?

A: I understand the term *institutional church* to mean a church that not only does the direct work of preaching the Gospel and building Christians up by teaching the Bible, but one that also looks after the physical and mental welfare of its members and congregation by various institutions. Such work is not necessarily detrimental to the real work of the church as set forth in the New Testament. It may be a valuable auxiliary, provided that the physical and intellectual are kept in thorough subordination to the spiritual.

The apostolic church was, in a measure, an institutional church. It looked out for the physical welfare of its members (Acts 6:1-5), all property was held in common (Acts 2:44-45; 4:34-35), and the Word of God increased and prospered under these circumstances (Acts 2:47; 4:4; 5:14; 6:7). Of course, the institutions were not many, nor were they very largely developed. In a similar way today, the church can have various institutions for looking after the physical and intellectual welfare of its members. If a church is located among the poor, it can offer financial counsel and assistance and can help people to heat their homes in the winter; it can provide libraries, educational classes, and so forth, accomplishing a vast amount of good, and making all this subservient to the preaching of the Gospel. All these things can be used as means of getting hold of men, women, and children and bringing them to a saving knowledge of Jesus Christ.

But there is always a danger in an institutional church. The danger is that the institutions will become the main thing and the Gospel will be put in a secondary place or will be lost sight of altogether. This has been the history of more than one institutional church in this country, and it is always a danger. In such a case, the institutional church becomes detrimental to the real work of the church as set forth in the New Testament. The first work of the church is seeking and saving the lost (Luke 19:10; Matthew 28:19–20). Its second work is the spiritual care of the congregation (Acts 20:28; 1 Peter 5:2–4), and its third work is training the membership for intelligent service (Ephesians 4:11–12). If the institutions connected with the church are allowed to put any one of these three things in the background, they do more harm than good. But if the institutions are carried on in the spirit of prayer and with the intention—never lost sight of for a moment—of winning men for Christ, and if everything is made subordinate to the preaching of the Gospel and the salvation of the lost and the edification of the saints, then the institutions may be very helpful.

Q: Is it ever right to ask unconverted though moral people to teach a Sunday school class or do other definite Christian work in the church?

A: *Ever* is a pretty comprehensive word. The ideal way is to have only thoroughly regenerated and spiritually-minded people teach a Sunday school class or sing in a choir. The church with which I

49

am connected takes the position that the very first condition of admission to membership in our choir is that the person applying must give good evidence of being born again. The second condition is that they have a good singing voice. But I can think of situations in which it would be warranted to have an unconverted person teach a Sunday school class. For example, suppose I were to go into a town to hold evangelistic meetings where there was no Sunday school and no religious work of any kind. If I could start a Sunday school there before I left, and get some moral person to teach the Bible—if there was no regenerated person available—I believe I would start the school and trust that the Spirit of God would use the Scripture as a blessing to both the teacher and the students. I would take the appointment of this person as a teacher as an opportunity to urge upon him the necessity of a personal acceptance of Christ.

I have held evangelistic meetings around the world, and the committees that organized the choirs for these meetings often received people who I do not believe were really converted. I have used the fact that they were in the choir as an opportunity of presenting the Gospel to them, and hundreds of people have thus been converted to God.

Q: What authority is there for or against women being prominent in the work of the church?

A: There is no authority given in the Bible for a woman to have the place of supremacy in the church. When she takes it, she steps out of her right place. She goes against the plain teaching of the Bible when she takes the place of the authoritative teacher in the church. *"And I do not permit a woman to teach or to have authority over a man, but to be in silence"* (1 Timothy 2:12).

However, there is abundant authorization in the Bible for a woman being active and, in that sense, prominent in church work. Women were the first divinely commissioned preachers of the risen Christ. Jesus Christ Himself sent them to declare His resurrection to the men disciples (John 20:17–18; Matthew 28:5–10). Women were endowed by God with prophetic gifts (Acts 21:9). It is significant that in the very book in the Bible in which women are forbidden to do idle talking and ask questions in the church (1 Corinthians 14:33–35), there are directions as to how a woman should prophesy, that is, how she should speak in the power of the Spirit (1 Corinthians 11:5). The apostle Paul spoke of the women who had labored with him in the Gospel (Philippians 4:3). There is clear indication that Priscilla was more gifted than her husband Aquila. She was associated with her husband in taking the preacher Apollos aside and expounding to him the way of God more accurately (Acts 18:24–26), and her name is mentioned first. (See NIV, NAS, and RV.)

Q: What is the scriptural way of raising money for church or other Christian uses?

A: The scriptural way of raising money is by the freewill offerings of saved people, each one setting aside on the first day of the week a definite proportion of his income (1 Corinthians 16:2). Certainly, it is not the scriptural way of raising money to raise it by fairs, bazaars, or any other method that reduces the church of Christ to the level of vaudeville entertainment. These methods are unwise even from a business standpoint, and they are certainly dishonoring to Jesus Christ. The successful churches are those that step out in obedience to the Word of God and depend upon the freewill offerings of the people. They soon find that they have more money for their own work and more money for missions than those churches that stoop to dishonor their Lord by raising money in such a way that it makes the church a reproach even among people of the world.

Q: Would you ask an unsaved person to contribute money or goods for the support or benefit of church work?

A: No, I would not. God is not dependent upon His enemies to help Him carry on His work. God's work should be supported by the joyful freewill offerings of His own people, as explained in the previous answer. Furthermore, when unsaved people contribute to the support of God's work, it frequently acts as a salve to their consciences, and it makes them harder to reach. They say, "I am supporting the church," and many of them hope to get to heaven in that way.

Of course, if some unsaved person, of his own volition, should see fit to put money into the collection, or something of that kind, I would hesitate to insult him by refusing his money. However, when offerings are taken, I would let it be clearly understood that it is not the money but the souls of the unsaved that we are seeking, and that men should first give themselves to the Lord before they give their money.

COMMUNION

Q: Should we invite to the Lord's Table all who believe themselves to be Christians, whether or not they have previously been received into the membership of the church?

A: Jesus Christ commands all believers, *"Do this in remembrance of Me"* (1 Corinthians 11:24). Therefore, all believers should have the privilege of doing this, whether or not they have previously been received into the membership of the church. But the importance and necessity of church membership should be urged upon all believers.

CONFESSION OF SINS

Q: Should we confess our sins to man or only to God?

A: First of all, we should confess them to God. David said in Psalm 32:5, *"I acknowledged my sin to You, and my iniquity I have not hidden. I said, 'I will confess my transgressions to the LORD,' and You forgave the iniquity of my sin."* In 1 John 1:9, we read: *"If we confess our sins* [and it clearly means, to God], *He is faithful and just to forgive us our sins and to cleanse us from all unrighteousness."*

However, if we have sinned against someone, we should confess our sin to the person against whom we have sinned. We should be reconciled to our brother who has something against us (Matthew 5:23–24). It is well also to confess our sins to one another so that we may pray for one another (James 5:16). There is not the slightest hint, however, that this means we should confess our sins to a priest any more than to any other brother. The verse says, *"Confess...to one another"* (v. 16). There is not any more reason why we should confess our sins to a priest than that the priest should confess his sins to us.

If we have sinned publicly, we should make public confession of our sins. But there is nothing in the Bible to indicate that one should make a detailed public confession of all his transgressions, or even that he should confess to any man every sin that he has committed. Religious impostors often require this of their disciples, and, in this way, they gain control over their disciples and rule them by fear of exposure. I know of one religious impostor who gained control over his people in this way. He made them confess everything base and vile that they had ever done; then he terrorized them, got their money from them, and made slaves of them. There are some things that a man should keep to himself and God.

CONSCIENCE

Q: Is the conscience a sufficient guide for man?

A: No. Conscience, using the word in the sense of the moral intuition that every person possesses that right is right and wrong is wrong, and that each of us ought to commit to following wherever it leads us, is sufficient to lead us to an absolute surrender to do what is right, whatever it may be. However, then there comes the question of what is right. Conscience, in the sense of moral judgment as to what is right or wrong, is certainly not a sufficient guide for man. Many people conscientiously do things that are utterly wrong because their moral judgment has been improperly educated. Conscience needs to be enlightened by divine revelation and by the personal illumination of the Holy Spirit as to what is right.

If we surrender ourselves to doing what is right, wherever it leads us, and if we make an honest search for what is right and true, we will be led to see that Jesus Christ is the Son of God and a Teacher sent from God. (See Matthew 16:16; John 3:2; 7:16–17.) Then we will bring our moral judgment to Him for education. Having accepted Jesus Christ as the Son of God and a Teacher sent from God, we will logically be led by the study of His Word to accept the entire Bible as the Word of God, and we will consequently take it as our guide in conduct. Furthermore, we will be led to see that it is our privilege to be taught by the Holy Spirit and to be guided into right conduct by Him.

CONSECRATION

Q: What is meant by "consecration"? How often should a person consecrate himself?

A: In today's usage (which, by the way, is not the way the Bible uses it), the word *consecration* means the surrendering of oneself and all that one has wholly to God. The word *sanctify,* as it is used in the Bible, has practically the same meaning when it is applied to sanctifying ourselves. It means to "set apart" for God.

Every Christian should consecrate himself to God once and for all. He should put into God's hands all that he is and all that he has, so that God may use him and everything that is his as He wills, send him where He wills, and do with him what He wills. Having thus consecrated himself, he should never take himself out of God's hands. However, many people do consecrate themselves to God and afterward go back on their consecration, as Samson did, and they are shorn of their strength, as Samson was. (See Judges 13:2–5; 16:1–19.) In such a case, a person should reconsecrate himself to God. Even when a person has not gone back on his consecration, it is a good thing to constantly re-acknowledge it so that one may keep it clearly in mind.

Furthermore, consecration gets a deeper significance the longer we live. At one time in our lives, we may wholly give ourselves up to God as far as we understand it at the time. However, as we study the Word and grow in grace, consecration will continually gain a deeper meaning. I believe I have been wholly God's for many years, but only yesterday I got a deeper understanding of what it means to be wholly God's than I have ever had before.

CONVICTION OF SIN

Q: How is conviction of sin produced? In other words, what kind of preaching would you recommend in order to bring people to a realization of the awfulness of sin, and to bring upon them conviction of sin?

A: The law was given to bring men to a knowledge of sin (Romans 3:20), and I find that the preaching of the law does bring men to such a knowledge. I preach on the Ten Commandments, looking to the Holy Spirit to show men how they have not kept them. I also preach on Matthew 7:12, the so-called Golden Rule, to show people that they have not kept the Golden Rule and therefore cannot be saved by it: *"Whatever you want men to do to you, do also to them."* In addition, I preach on Matthew 22:37–38. Through these verses, I seek to show people that they have not only sinned but they have also broken the first and greatest of God's commandments: *"'You shall love the LORD your God with all your heart, with all your soul, and with all your mind.' This is the first and great commandment."*

However, we read in John 16:8–9 that the sin of which the Holy Spirit convicts men is the sin of unbelief in Jesus Christ. Also, we see in Acts 2:1–37 that the sin of which the Holy Spirit convicted so many thousands on the Day of Pentecost was the sin of rejecting Jesus Christ. Working along these lines, I find that holding up before men the majesty and glory of Jesus Christ and the sacrifice He made for us, then driving home the awfulness of the sin of rejecting such a Savior, brings the deepest conviction of sin.

But in all our preaching, we must bear in mind that it is the Holy Spirit, not we ourselves, who convicts men of sin. He does it through the truth that we present, but we must realize our dependence upon Him and look to Him and count on Him to do the work. This is where many make their mistake. They try to convict men of sin instead of putting themselves in an attitude of complete dependence on the Holy Spirit so that He will convict men through them.

THE DEITY OF JESUS CHRIST

Q: How would you prove that Jesus Christ is really the Son of God?

A: First, I would prove that He rose from the dead. Of this there is abundant proof. I have given it elsewhere and will not repeat it here.* The fact that Jesus Christ rose from the dead proves beyond a question that He is the Son of God.

When He was here on earth, He repeatedly declared that He was the Son of God—the Son of God in a unique sense, the Son of God in a sense in which no other man is the Son of God. In Mark 12:1–6, Jesus taught that while the prophets, even the greatest of them, were servants, He was a Son,

---

*See R. A. Torrey, *Powerful Faith* (New Kensington, PA: Whitaker House, 1996).

an only Son. In John 5:22–23, He taught that all men should honor Him even as they honor the Father. In John 14:9, He went so far as to say, *"He who has seen Me has seen the Father."* Men hated Him for making this claim to be the Son of God; they put Him to death for making this claim (Matthew 26:63–66). However, before they put Him to death, He told them that God would set His seal on the claim by raising Him from the dead. (See John 2:19.) It was a stupendous claim to make; it was an apparently absurd claim, but God did set His seal on it by raising Jesus from the dead. By doing this, God Himself has spoken more clearly than if He spoke from the open heavens today, "This Man is what He claims to be. He is My Son. All men should honor Him even as they honor the Father."

To summarize the first point, Jesus Christ proved Himself to be the Son of God by the claim He made to be the Son of God and by the way in which He substantiated that claim by His resurrection from the dead.

Second, He substantiated His claim by His character, by its beauty and strength and nobility. The character of Jesus Christ is nearly universally acknowledged. Jews nowadays acknowledge it. Even the most notorious infidels have admitted it. Robert Green Ingersoll once said, "I wish to say once and for all, to that great and serene Man I gladly pay the homage of my admiration and my tears." But here is this Man, whom all admit to be a good man, a man of honor and truth and nobility, claiming to be the Son of God. Certainly a Man of such character was what He claimed to be.

Third, He substantiated His claim by the miracles that He performed. Herculean efforts have been put forth to discredit the gospel accounts of Christ's miracles, but these efforts have all resulted in utter failure. He substantiated His claim by His influence on the history of the world. No argument is needed to prove that Christ's influence on the history of the world has done immeasurably more good than that of any other man who ever lived. It would be foolish to compare His influence on individual life, domestic life, social life, industrial life, and political life with that of any other man, or that of all men put together. Now, if Jesus Christ was not divine, as He claimed to be, He was a blasphemer and an impostor or else a lunatic. It is easy to see that His influence on history is not that of a lunatic or a blasphemer and an impostor. Then, certainly, He must have been the Son of God as He claimed.

Fourth, I would prove that Jesus Christ is the Son of God by pointing to the fact that He possesses divine power today. It is not necessary to go back to the miracles that Christ performed when He was on earth to prove that He has divine power. He exercises that power today, and anyone can test it. There are two major ways in which His power is demonstrated today:

In the first place, He has power to forgive sins. Thousands can testify that they came to Christ burdened with a terrible sense of guilt and that He has actually given their guilty consciences peace, absolute peace.

Moreover, He has power today to set Satan's victims free. He sets the one chained by drink free from the power of drink, the one chained by drugs free from the power of drugs. You may say that various medical treatments also do this, but the cases are not parallel. These various treatments use drugs; Christ uses a mere word. Christ sets people free not only from vices but also from other sin. He makes the impure man pure. He makes the selfish man unselfish. He makes the devilish man Christlike. He re-creates men and women. The divine influence that Jesus Christ is exerting today over the lives of countless men and women proves beyond a doubt that He is the Son of God. I know that Jesus Christ is divine because of the divine work that He, and He alone, has worked in my own life.

THE DEPRAVITY OF MAN

Q: What do you mean by the doctrine of the total depravity of man, and how do you prove it?

A: The doctrine that man is totally depraved does not mean that he is totally corrupt. It means that the will of the unregenerate man is set upon pleasing self and is therefore totally wrong, for it should be set upon pleasing God. The will that is not absolutely surrendered to God is turned the wrong way. Yet while seeking to please himself, a man may do things that are morally attractive and beautiful. A man is not necessarily drawn to immoral and disgusting things. He may prefer things that are high and noble and true, yet he may not prefer them because they are what God wills but because they are the things that attract him. He is as truly depraved as the man who chooses the immoral things, but his tastes are not as corrupt as those of the man who chooses immoral things. What every unregenerate man needs is a total turning around of his will, so that he no longer seeks to please himself but surrenders himself in all things to do the things that please God and to do them because they please God.

The doctrine of total depravity may be proved first by the Scriptures. For example, consider these verses, as well as many other Scriptures: *"The carnal mind is enmity against God; for it is not subject to the law of God, nor indeed can be"* (Romans 8:7). *"Having their understanding darkened, being alienated from the life of God, because of the ignorance that is in them, because of the blindness of their heart"* (Ephesians 4:18). *"The heart is deceitful above all things, and desperately wicked"* (Jeremiah 17:9).

The doctrine of the total depravity of man may also be proved by an appeal to facts. The picture of the unregenerate man given in the Scriptures at first sight seems to be too dark. However, as we come to know men better—especially as we come to know ourselves better, and above all as we come to know God better and see ourselves in the light of His holiness—this Bible doctrine is found to be absolutely accurate.

THE DEVIL

Q: Do you believe in a real Devil—one that has the qualities of a person, such as a personality and a will? Or is he merely a metaphor for evil?

A: Most assuredly, I believe in a real Devil. I could not believe in the Bible without believing in a real Devil. In another book, I give conclusive proof that the Bible is the Word of God.* Therefore, I believe what it teaches about the existence of a Devil.

In the accounts of the temptation of our Lord, recorded in the gospels of Matthew and Luke, we are distinctly told that the Devil (and the accounts clearly mean a personal Devil) was the author of the temptations that came to our Lord. (See Matthew 4:1–11; Luke 4:1–13.) These accounts have no meaning if we try to make the Devil of these passages a mere metaphor for evil.

Furthermore, in the parable of the sower (Matthew 13:1–23), our Lord distinctly taught

*See R. A. Torrey, *Powerful Faith* (New Kensington, PA: Whitaker House, 1996).

that there is a real Devil. The Devil does not appear in the parable, where he might be explained as being figurative, but rather in the interpretation of the parable: *"Then the wicked one comes"* (v. 19). Now, in parables we have symbolic language, and in the interpretation of parables we have the literal facts for which the symbols stand. Therefore, we have a literal Devil in the interpretation of this parable. This is only one of the numerous instances in which Jesus taught the existence of a real Devil.

The apostle Paul taught the same. For example, in Ephesians 6:11–12, he wrote, *"Put on the whole armor of God, that you may be able to stand against the wiles of the devil. For we do not wrestle against flesh and blood, but against principalities, against powers, against the rulers of the darkness of this age, against spiritual hosts of wickedness in the heavenly places."*

No rational interpretation of the Bible can interpret the Devil out of it. Any system of interpretation that does away with the Devil would do away with any doctrine that a person does not wish to believe.

I also believe that there is a real Devil because my own experience and observation teach me the existence of an unseen, very subtle, very cunning spirit of evil, who has domination over men throughout human society. The more I come into contact with men, the more I study history, and the more men open their hearts to me, the more firmly convinced I become that there is a Devil such as the Bible teaches.

It is not pleasant to believe that there is a real Devil, but the question is not what is pleasant to believe, but what is true.

Q: Why did God create the Devil, also called Satan?

A: God created Satan because God is love. God created him whom we now call Satan as a being of very exalted glory. In Ezekiel 28:12–15, we get a hint of what Satan was when he was originally created: *"You were the seal of perfection, full of wisdom and perfect in beauty. You were in Eden, the garden of God; every precious stone was your covering: the sardius, topaz, and diamond, beryl, onyx, and jasper, sapphire, turquoise, and emerald with gold. The workmanship of your timbrels and pipes was prepared for you on the day you were created. You were the anointed cherub who covers; I established you; you were on the holy mountain of God; you walked back and forth in the midst of fiery stones. You were perfect in your ways from the day you were created, till iniquity was found in you."*

Because he was a being of such exalted glory, he was a moral being, that is, a being with the power of choosing good or evil. He seems to have been the one who led the worship of the universe. But ambition entered his heart. He seems to have tried to direct to himself what properly belonged to God, and thus he fell. Falling from such a height, he fell to the deepest depths and became the appalling being that he now is. The Devil of Scripture is not a hideous-looking being with horns and hoofs, but a being of very high intelligence who has turned his mighty powers to wrong and has thus become the great enemy of God and man.

Q: Can God destroy Satan?

A: I do not know of anywhere in the Bible where it is taught that God can destroy Satan, but God certainly can destroy or annihilate any beings that He has created, if He sees fit. If He brought them into being, He can put them out of being; otherwise, God would not be omnipotent. But it is clear from Scripture that to destroy Satan is not God's will. Satan will exist and be *"tormented day and night forever and ever"* (Revelation 20:10). If the question refers to Hebrews 2:14— *"through death He...destroy*[ed] *him who had the power of death, that is, the devil"*—the word *"destroy"* there means to "render powerless" or "bring to nothing," not "annihilate." (See NAS and RV.)

Q: Why does God not destroy Satan if He is omnipotent?

A: God does not destroy Satan because God has not yet worked out His purposes through him. Though Satan himself is evil, God accomplishes His purposes of good through him. The day will come when we will understand what these purposes are and will thank God even for Satan. God will make not only the wrath of man but also the wrath of Satan to praise Him. (See Psalm 76:10.) The *"messenger of Satan"* that was sent to *"buffet"* Paul (2 Corinthians 12:7) worked only good for Paul. He kept Paul from being *"exalted above measure"* (v. 7).

DIVORCE

Q: Does the Bible permit a person, under any circumstances, to divorce his or her spouse and marry another while the divorced spouse is still living?

A: It is perfectly clear that the Bible does not permit divorce and remarriage on any grounds but one. It says, *"Whoever divorces his wife for any reason except sexual immorality causes her to commit adultery"* (Matthew 5:32). Moreover, if the one who gets the divorce marries another, he or she also commits adultery (19:9). This much is as plain as day, namely, that there is only one scriptural basis for divorce and remarriage: impurity on the part of the other party.

Divorce and remarriage are, however, objected to by some who believe that remarriage even on this ground is not permitted by Scripture—that in Romans 7:2–3, it is stated without any exception that a *"woman who has a husband is bound by the law to her husband as long as he lives"* and that *"if, while her husband lives, she marries another man, she will be called an adulteress."* The answer to this objection seems evident. Paul in Romans 7 was not discussing the question of divorce but was simply using the matter of the marriage obligation as an illustration. Paul was making a point about death in this passage. It would have been entirely out of Paul's way for him to have gone into the matter of exceptions to the general law, as they had no bearing whatsoever on the question that he was discussing. The words of Christ clearly seem to imply that in this one case of infidelity, a man may divorce his wife and marry another, and be guiltless before God.

It would seem, however, that if a person has divorced an unfaithful partner, it would be better for the person to remain single, at least until the death of the offending party, and thus avoid *"troubles in this life"* (1 Corinthians 7:28). But if a person has divorced a spouse on the ground of adultery and has already married another, there is no scriptural reason why he or she should feel guilty.

ETERNAL PUNISHMENT

Q: Do you believe in the eternal punishment of the wicked? What proof is there of eternal punishment?

A: We know nothing positively and absolutely about the future except what God Himself has been pleased to reveal in His Word. Everything beyond this is pure speculation, and man's speculations on such a subject are practically valueless. God knows all about the future, and He has been pleased to reveal some things that He knows about the future. On such a subject as this, an ounce of God's revelation is worth tons of man's empty speculation. God has clearly revealed in the Bible the fact of eternal punishment for those who persist in sin and in the rejection of Jesus Christ, and this is conclusive proof of its reality. I have shown in another book that the Bible is unquestionably the Word of God.* The Bible tells us what God says, and the Bible distinctly teaches that there will be an eternity of punishment for those who persistently reject the redemption that is in Christ Jesus. Consider these verses: *"Depart from Me, you cursed, into the everlasting fire prepared for the devil and his angels....These will go away into everlasting punishment, but the righteous into eternal life"* (Matthew 25:41, 46). *"Then the beast was captured, and with him the false prophet who worked signs in his presence, by which he deceived those who received the mark of the beast and those who worshiped his image. These two were cast alive into the lake of fire burning with brimstone....The devil, who deceived them, was cast into the lake of*

---

*See R. A. Torrey, *Powerful Faith* (New Kensington, PA: Whitaker House, 1996).

fire and brimstone where the beast and the false prophet are. And they will be tormented day and night forever and ever....But the cowardly, unbelieving, abominable, murderers, sexually immoral, sorcerers, idolaters, and all liars shall have their part in the lake which burns with fire and brimstone, which is the second death" (Revelation 19:20; 20:10; 21:8).

The expression *"forever and ever,"* used here of the lake of fire prepared for the Devil and his angels, to which the persistently wicked will also go, is used thirteen times in the book of Revelation. Nine times it refers to the duration of the existence or reign or glory of God and Christ, once to the duration of the blessed reign of the righteous, and in the three remaining instances to the duration of the torment of the Devil, the Beast, the False Prophet, and the persistently wicked.

Q: Does the Bible teach that there will be eternal torment for all of the unsaved? If so, where?

A: The Bible teaches in 2 Thessalonians 1:7–9 that when the Lord Jesus is revealed from heaven, all those who do not know God and do not obey the Gospel of our Lord Jesus Christ will be *"punished with everlasting destruction from the presence of the Lord and from the glory of His power"* (v. 9). The question then arises, what does *"destruction"* mean? The Bible itself defines the term. We are told in the eighth and eleventh verses of Revelation 17 that the Beast will go to *"perdition."* (See KJV, NKJV, RV.) The word rendered *"perdition,"* the same word that is elsewhere translated "destruction," is derived from the verb that is constantly translated "destroy." The word *"perdition"* should therefore be translated "destruction" in this passage in Revelation. So then, if we can find out what the Beast will go to, we will find out what *"perdition"* or "destruction" means. By turning to Revelation 19:20, we find that the Beast will be cast alive into *"the lake of fire burning with brimstone."* Turning again to Revelation 20:10, we find that at the end of a thousand years, after the Beast has been cast into the lake burning with brimstone, the Devil will be cast into the lake burning with fire and brimstone, where the Beast and the False Prophet still are after the thousand years, and that they will be *"tormented day and night forever and ever."* So then, this is what "destruction" means in Bible usage: a share in the lake of fire. Whether this is taken literally or figuratively, it certainly means a condition of being in a place of conscious and unending torment.

Q: How could a loving God create some of His creatures for eternal punishment?

A: God did not create any of His creatures for eternal punishment. God created all people to love and obey Him and enjoy Him forever. But He also created them as a higher order of beings, with the capacity of choosing for themselves good or evil. Some chose evil. However, even then, God did not abandon them but made the greatest sacrifice in His power to save them from their own mad choice. He gave His Son to die for them so that repentance, forgiveness, life, and glory might be possible for them. If men see fit not only to choose evil but also, having chosen evil, to deliberately and persistently refuse the means of salvation that a loving God has provided for them at immeasurable cost to Himself, then their eternal punishment is their own fault. To blame God for it is not only to be appallingly unjust but also unpardonably ungrateful and unreasonable.

Q: How can an infinitely holy and merciful God condemn creatures He loves to everlasting punishment?

A: It is not so much that God condemns anyone to everlasting punishment as that men and women condemn themselves to everlasting torment by refusing the mercy and grace of God. Many people not only choose sin but also choose to refuse the wonderfully gracious redemption from sin that God has provided. If people will not allow themselves to be saved from sin, they must necessarily continue in it; and if they continue in it, they must necessarily suffer torment as long as they continue in it. The time must come, sooner or later, when repentance becomes impossible, and so, of course, salvation becomes impossible. The everlasting torment that anyone may endure will be simply the inevitable result of his own deliberate and persistent choice of sin.

Q: Is it not unjust to punish a few years of sin with an eternity of torment?

A: The duration of the punishment of sin can never be determined by the time it takes to commit the sin. A man can kill another man in a few seconds, but a just penalty would be lifelong imprisonment. Furthermore, sin involves separation from God, and separation from God is torment. The torment must continue as long as the separation from God exists, and the separation from God must exist until sin is repented of and the Savior is accepted. The time must come when repentance and the acceptance of the Savior become impossible; then one becomes eternally confirmed in his separation from God, and eternal torment must necessarily follow.

In addition, it is not a few years of sin that bring the eternity of punishment. A man may continue many years in sin and still escape eternal torment if he will only repent and accept Jesus Christ. It is the rejection of Jesus Christ that brings an eternity of torment. When we see sin in all its hideousness and enormity, the holiness of God in all its perfection, and the glory of Jesus Christ in all its infinity, nothing will satisfy the demand of our own moral intuitions except eternal punishment for those who persist in the choice of sin and in the rejection of the Son of God. This is especially so when we consider the fact that God, in His wonderful grace, gave Christ Jesus to die for our sins so that we might have salvation. Moreover, it is the fact that we dread suffering more than we hate sin and more than we love the glory of Jesus Christ that makes us reject the thought of eternal punishment for those who eternally choose sin, despise God's mercy, and spurn His Son.

Q: Would an earthly father send his child to everlasting suffering? And if he would not, can we believe that God is not as good as we are and that He would treat His children in a way that we would not treat ours?

A: First, this question takes it for granted that all men are God's children. The Bible teaches that this is not true. All men are God's creatures and were originally created in His likeness, and in this sense they are all His offspring (Acts 17:26–29). But men become God's children in the fullest sense by being born again of the Holy Spirit (John 3:3–6) through the personal acceptance of Jesus Christ as their Savior (John 1:12; Galatians 3:26).

Second, God is something besides the Father, even to believers. He is the moral Governor of this universe. As a righteous moral Governor of the universe, He must punish sin; consequently, if sin is eternally persisted in, He must eternally punish it. Even a wise earthly father would separate one of his own children who persisted in sin from contact with his other children. If a man had a dearly beloved son who was a moral monster, he certainly would not allow him to associate with his daughters. If a person whom you greatly loved committed a gross wrong against someone you loved more, and persisted in it eternally, would you not consent to his eternal punishment?

Third, it is never safe to measure what an infinitely holy God would do by what we would do. As we look about us in the world today, do we not see men and women suffering agonies that we would not allow our children to suffer if we could prevent it? Which of us could endure to see our children suffering some of the things that the men and women in the slums of the cities are suffering today? It may be difficult for us to explain why a God of love permits this to go on, but we know that it does go on. Moreover, what men and women suffer in this present life as a result of their disobedience to God and their persistence in sin and their rejection of Jesus Christ ought to be a hint of what people will suffer in the eternal world if they go on in sin as the result of their having rejected the Savior in this present life. It may sound good to say, "I believe in a God of love, and I do not believe that He will permit any of His creatures to go to an eternal hell." However, if we open our eyes to the facts as they exist everywhere around us, we will see how empty our speculations on this point are, for even now we see this same God of love permitting many of His creatures to endure terrible and ever increasing agonies in this present life.

Q: If anyone is lost eternally, has not Satan then gained the victory over Christ, and is he not stronger than Christ?

A: No, Satan has gained no victory. It is not Satan who determines that a person will persist in sin; it is the individual himself. If he persists in sin, Satan has gained no victory, and, on the other hand, Jesus Christ is not conquered. Jesus Christ will still be glorified, and God will be glorified. God's holiness is manifested and God Himself is glorified as truly in the punishment of the sinner as in the salvation of the believer. Righteous government here on earth is vindicated as truly when the offender is locked up in prison or executed as when the offender is brought to repentance.

Many seem to think that hell is a place ruled by Satan, but Satan does not rule there. Satan himself will be one of the prisoners, and the smoke of the torment of this persistent rebel against God will rise forever and ever as a testimony that God has conquered him.

EVIL

Q: How can God permit evil to exist in the world?

A: When we enter the domain of asking how God can do this or that, we need to tread very softly, for God is a Being of infinite wisdom, and we know almost nothing. When we think about how vast God is and how infinitesimal we are, we do well to hesitate about questioning how God can do anything. An infinitely wise God may have a thousand good reasons for doing things, when we, in our almost utter ignorance, cannot see one good or even possible reason for them.

Having said this much, I may add that evil seems to be a necessary accompaniment of good. Moral good is the highest good, and freedom of choice is necessary for the attainment of moral good. In fact, no being can be good in the highest sense unless it is possible for him to do evil; but if it is possible for him to do evil, he may do it. God created all beings good, but the highest beings were created with the power of choice. They could choose disobedience to God if they desired. One of the very highest of such beings, he whom we now call Satan, chose evil. God created man with the power of choice also, and the first man chose evil, and the whole race followed him. Thus evil entered into the world as the outcome of God's having created man on the highest plane, that is, with the lofty power of choice.

God will permit evil to continue in the world until He has fully worked out His own benevolent plans. When we come to see no longer *"through a glass, darkly; but...face to face"* (1 Corinthians 13:12 KJV), we will undoubtedly rejoice that God did permit evil to exist in the world.

FAITH

Q: What do you mean by "justification by faith"? Is faith the only means of salvation?

A: The Greek word that is translated "to justify" in the New Testament would, according to its word origin, mean "to make righteous." However, this meaning is extremely rare in Greek usage, if not altogether doubtful, and it certainly is not the New Testament usage of the word. In biblical usage, "to justify" does not signify "to make righteous" but "to reckon, declare, or show to be righteous." A person is justified before God when God reckons him righteous, that is, when God not only forgives his sins but also credits all "positive righteousness" to his account. This means that when God justifies us, He not only cleanses us from the sins that we have committed against Him (sins of commission) but also credits to our account all the good works that we should have done but failed to do (sins of omission).

There is one condition upon which men are justified before God: simple faith in Jesus Christ. (See Romans 3:26; 4:5; 5:1; Acts 13:39.) It is the atoning death of Jesus Christ on the cross in our place that secures justification for us. (See Romans 5:9; Galatians 3:13; 2 Corinthians 5:21.) His shed blood is the ground of our justification, and simple faith in Him makes that shed blood ours. Provision is made for our justification by the shedding of His blood; we are actually justified when we believe in Him who shed His blood. Faith is the only means of securing for ourselves the atoning power that there is in the blood of Jesus Christ. If a person will not believe, there is nothing he can do that will bring him justification.

If a person does believe, he is absolved from *"all things"* the moment he believes (Acts 13:38–39). Not only are all his sins put out of God's sight, but in God's reckoning, all of God's own righteousness in Jesus Christ is also credited to his account. When Jesus Christ died on the cross of Calvary, He took our place (Galatians 3:10, 13), and the moment we believe in Him, we step into His place and are just as pleasing to God as Jesus Christ Himself is.

Q: I would like to believe, but I cannot. Will God condemn me for something I cannot do?

A: No, God will not condemn you for something you cannot do, but you can believe. Anyone can believe. There is plenty of proof that the Bible is the Word of God and that Jesus Christ is the Son of God—proof enough to convince anyone who really wants to know and obey the truth.

In my book *Powerful Faith*,* I have given conclusive evidence that the Bible is God's Word and

---

*See R. A. Torrey, *Powerful Faith* (New Kensington, PA: Whitaker House, 1996).

that Jesus Christ is God's Son. However, one does not need to read books like this to find this evidence. There is plenty of proof in the Bible itself. John said in John 20:31, *"These are written* [the things contained in the gospel of John] *that you may believe that Jesus is the Christ, the Son of God, and that believing you may have life in His name."* We see in this verse that life comes through believing that Jesus is the Christ, the Son of God, and that believing that Jesus is the Christ, the Son of God, comes through studying what is written. If anyone will take the gospel of John and read it in the right way, he will know and believe before he finishes reading that Jesus is the Christ, the Son of God, and he will have life through believing it.

Now, what is the right way to read it?

♦ First of all, surrender your will to God. Jesus said, *"If anyone chooses to do God's will, he will find out whether my teaching comes from God or whether I speak on my own"* (John 7:17 NIV). One can read the gospel of John again and again and not come to believe that Jesus is the Christ, the Son of God, if he reads it with an unsurrendered will. However, if a person will first surrender his will to God to obey God, no matter what it may cost him, he cannot read the gospel of John through once without coming to see that Jesus is the Christ, the Son of the living God.

♦ Second, each time you read the Bible, look to God and ask Him to show you how much truth there is in the verses you are about to read. Then promise Him that you will commit to what He shows you is true. Do not read too many verses at once. Pay careful attention to what you read. Read with a real desire to learn the truth and to obey it. By the time you get through the gospel, you will find that you can believe. In fact, you will find that you do believe.

The reason people do not believe is that they are not living up to what they do believe, they have not surrendered their wills to God, or they do not study the evidence that is intended to produce belief. Men neglect their Bibles and read all kinds of trashy, unbelieving books and then keep saying, "I can't believe! I can't believe!" A man might just as well feed himself on poison instead of food and then complain that he is not healthy. There is abundant evidence that Jesus Christ is the Son of God, and faith is a willingness to yield to sufficient evidence—it is a matter of the will. Unbelief is the refusal to yield to sufficient evidence. Unbelief is a matter for which every unbeliever is responsible.

God demands that we believe, that we yield our wills to the truth that He has abundantly revealed. Faith is the one thing that God demands of man, because it is the one thing above all else that we owe to God (John 6:29). Without the faith that is due to God, it is impossible to please Him (Hebrews 11:6).

FALLING FROM GRACE

Q: How do you harmonize the Calvinistic view of the perseverance of the saints with the Arminian belief that one may fall from grace?

A: If I understand the Calvinistic view, it does not teach the perseverance of the saints but the perseverance of the Savior. While it teaches that the saints are utterly unreliable and might fall away any day or any hour, it also teaches that the Savior is ever watchful and ever faithful. *"Therefore He is also able to save to the uttermost those who come to God through Him, since He always lives to make intercession for them"* (Hebrews 7:25). The Calvinist view teaches that the Savior has pledged that those who believe in Him will never perish (John 10:28). He has given His word that He and His Father will keep us to the end and that no man is able to snatch us out of the hand of Himself and the Father (vv. 28–29).

This does not mean that if a man is born again and then returns to live in sin that he will not be lost forever. It means that Jesus Christ will see to it that the one who is born again will not go back and live in sin. He may fall into sin—he may fall into gross sin—but Jesus Christ has undertaken his recovery. He will go after the lost sheep until He finds it (Luke 15:4). There is no warrant here for someone to continue in sin, saying, "I am a child of God and therefore cannot be lost." There is no comfort here whatsoever for such a person. If a person returns to living in sin and continues in sin, it is proof that he is not a child of God, is not saved, and never was regenerate. (See 1 John 2:19; 3:6, 9; 5:18.)

What the Arminians object to is not the doctrine of the faithfulness of the Savior—that He will prove true even though we prove faithless. What they object to is a doctrine such as "once in grace, always in grace" that enables a man to go on sinning and seeking to justify himself by saying, "I have been saved; therefore, I have been in grace and am still in grace."

On the one hand, we need to be on our guard against the doctrine that gives us comfort in continuance in sin. On the other hand, we need to be on our guard against a distrust of Jesus Christ that makes us fear that sometime we will prove unfaithful and Jesus Christ will desert us. The position we ought to hold is the one held by the apostle Paul. He asserted, on the one hand, *"I know whom I have believed and am persuaded that He is able to keep what I have committed to Him until that Day"* (2 Timothy 1:12). On the other hand, he was led to discipline his body (figuratively, to give his body a black eye) lest, when he had preached to others, he himself should become disqualified (1 Corinthians 9:27). (For a related topic, please refer to the section "The Unpardonable Sin" in this book.)

FASTING

Q: Should Christians fast?

A: Yes, Christians should do anything in their power that will bring blessing to themselves or others. Beyond a doubt, in many instances fasting brings blessings to the one who fasts as well as to others.

It is sometimes said that fasting belonged to the Jewish religion but not to the Christian. However, this contradicts the plain teaching of the Bible. In Acts 13:2, we are told that it was while they *"ministered to the Lord and fasted"* that the Holy Spirit spoke to the leaders of the church in Antioch. In the third verse, we are told that it was after they had *"fasted and prayed"* that they laid their hands on Saul and Barnabas and sent them off for the work to which Jesus had called them. In Acts 14:23, we are told that at the ordination of elders, they *"prayed with fasting."*

There is no virtue in a person's going without his necessary food. However, there is power in humbling ourselves before God by fasting because we have an acute awareness of our own unworthiness. There is power in a complete earnestness in seeking the face of God that leads us away from even our necessary food so that we may give ourselves up to prayer.

If there were more fasting and prayer and less feasting and frivolousness in the church of Jesus Christ today, we would see more revivals and more wonderful things worked for God.

FOOTWASHING

Q: Why do Christians not generally wash each others' feet as commanded in John 13:3–17?

A: There is no commandment in this passage that every Christian should wash every other Christian's feet. Nor is there today any church in which every Christian washes every other Christian's feet. There is a command here that when some other Christian needs to have his feet washed (John 13:10), we should be ready to perform even so menial a service as this for him, and thus do as Jesus did to His disciples in their need.

There is not the slightest indication that Jesus was appointing a ceremony to be performed in the church. The disciples had come in from the road with their feet dusty. The passage implies that they had bathed earlier in the day (see verses 9–10), and therefore did not need a total cleansing, but because they were wearing open sandals, their feet had become dusty along the way and needed to be washed. Yet each one of them was too proud to wash the other disciples' feet. There was no servant present to do it, so Jesus, though He knew He had come from the Father and was going to the Father, and that the Father had given all things into His hands (v. 3), rose from the table and performed for them the menial service that was needed.

Jesus' action has no resemblance whatsoever to the mere performance of the ceremony of washing feet that do not need to be washed, solely for the sake of doing the same thing that Jesus did. The lesson of the passage is plain enough, namely, that we ought to have the kind of love for one another that makes us ready to perform the lowliest service for one another.

FORGIVENESS OF SINS

Q: What does John 20:23 mean: *"If you forgive the sins of any, they are forgiven them; if you retain the sins of any, they are retained"*? Does this passage teach that the priest has power on earth to forgive sins?

A: The meaning of the verse is very clear if you notice exactly what is said and the exact context in which Jesus said it. In the preceding verse, Jesus had breathed on the disciples and said to them, *"Receive the Holy Spirit"* (v. 22). Then He said to them, *"If you forgive the sins of any, they are forgiven them; if you retain the sins of any, they are* *retained.*" In other words, Jesus taught that a disciple who had received the Holy Spirit would receive the power of spiritual discernment, through which he would know whether there had been true repentance or not, and whatever person's sins this Spirit-filled disciple pronounced were forgiven, were indeed forgiven.

The promise was not made to an official priest but to disciples who had been filled with the Holy Spirit. If a priest were filled with the Holy Spirit, he undoubtedly would receive this spiritual discernment. However, a man who is not a priest, except in the sense that all believers are priests (see Revelation 1:6), and who receives the Holy Spirit may have this spiritual discernment. There are times when any Spirit-filled person may know that a pretense of repentance that another person makes is not genuine; because of this, he may declare to that person that his sins are not forgiven, and indeed that person's sins are not forgiven. On other occasions, he may see that repentance and faith are genuine, and declare to the person that his sins are forgiven.

The apostle Peter, filled with the Holy Spirit, exercised this power in Acts 8:20–23. The apostle Paul, filled with the Holy Spirit, exercised it in Acts 13:9–11. Many humble believers have this Spirit-given discernment today. There is no mention whatsoever of priests in the passage, and there is absolutely nothing that can be built upon to prove that the priest as such has power on earth to forgive sins.

GIVING

Q: Do you believe in tithing your income for religious purposes?

A: Yes, as the starting point in Christian giving.

Q: What is the biblical standard for a Christian in the matter of giving money for religious work?

A: The Christian is not under any particular law in the matter of giving. That is to say, there is no absolute law laid down in the Bible that a Christian should give just so much and no more. However, a Christian should consecrate all that he has to God. Every penny of his money should belong to Him. The money he spends on himself and his family should be spent for that purpose because he thinks God would be more honored if he spent it in that way than in some other way.

In the Old Testament, the Jew was under the law to give one-tenth of his income, and, over and above that, he was expected to give freewill offerings. This Jewish law should be a suggestion to us as to where we should begin our giving. We should begin by giving one-tenth to Christ. But a Christian should not stop with a tenth. He should seek guidance as to the use of every penny he has in addition to the tenth.

Many who follow the plan of giving one-tenth have found great blessing in it. In fact, after they have set apart one-tenth to the Lord, many people have experienced a prosperity in their businesses that they never knew before. Most Christians who do not systematically give a tenth believe that they are giving more than a tenth. However, when they start setting apart a tenth of their income for the Lord, they discover that in the past they actually had been giving less than a tenth but that now they are giving much more than they ever have.

The "rule of three" given by the apostle Paul to the Corinthian church in connection with the collection for the poor Christians in Jerusalem is a simple but effective guideline for giving. It is found in 1 Corinthians 16:2: "[1] *On the first day of every week,* [2] *each one of you should set aside a sum of money* [3] *in keeping with his income"* (NIV).

Q: Does Matthew 5:42, *"Give to him who asks you, and from him who wants to borrow from you do not turn away,"* teach that a Christian should give to everyone who asks him for money if he has it in his pocket?

A: Matthew 5:42 undoubtedly teaches that the disciple of Jesus Christ should give to everyone who asks of him, but it does not teach that he should necessarily give money. When Peter and John were appealed to by the lame man at the Gate Beautiful, they gave to him, but they did not give him money. Instead, they gave him something better. (See Acts 3:2–8.) Paul distinctly said in 2 Thessalonians 3:10, *"If anyone will not work, neither shall he eat."* This does not mean that if a man is a tramp, we should not give to him when he asks, but it does mean that we should use discernment in what we give him.

Almost immediately following Matthew 5:42, Jesus tells us to be like our heavenly Father who *"makes His sun rise on the evil and on the good, and sends rain on the just and on the unjust"* (v. 45). Our giving should be patterned after our heavenly Father's. He gives to everyone who asks, but He does not always give exactly what they ask for.

GOD

Q: Do the names *God*, *Lord*, and *Lord God* all mean the same person—God?

A: Yes, in the Old Testament they do. They are different names of the Deity that stand for different conceptions of Him. For example, the name *God* is the more general name of the Deity. The name *LORD*, printed in small capitals and the equivalent of "Jehovah," is the name of God used when referring to Him as the covenant God of Israel.

The name *Lord* is generally used of Jesus in the New Testament.

There is a school of critics who want us to think that the use of these different names of the Deity indicates a different authorship of the different portions of Scripture where the names are used. This, for a long time, was the favorite argument of the destructive critics. For example, they tried to prove that the Pentateuch (the first five books of the Old Testament) was a patchwork of portions written by different men, but this argument has been thoroughly discredited.

The names of God are very carefully used in the Bible and make an interesting and profitable study.

Q: How would you prove the existence of God to an inquirer?

A: It would depend somewhat upon the inquirer. If he was an earnest seeker after truth, I would pursue one line of reasoning. If he was a mere trifler, I would pursue another.

In general, I would ask a person what he did believe. I would ask him specifically, "Do you believe there is an absolute difference between right and wrong?" In 999 cases out of 1,000, he would answer, "Yes." Then I would say to him, "The way to get more spiritual light is to live up to the light you have; the way to get more truth is to live up to the truth you have. You say you believe there is an absolute difference between right and wrong. Will you live up to that? Will you commit yourself to following this belief wherever it leads you?"

Very likely, he would try to dodge the question, but I would hold him to it. If he finally said, "No," then I would say to him, "The trouble with you is not in regard to what you do not believe, but, in fact, it is that you do not live up to what you do believe." He would see this and be silenced.

If he said that he would commit himself to following it wherever it led him, I would next say, "Do you know for certain that there is not a God?" Of course, he would answer, "No." Then I would ask, "Do you know for certain that God does not answer prayer?" Very likely, he would answer, "I do not know for certain that He does not answer prayer, but I do not believe He does." I would answer, "I know that He does, but that will not do you any good. I will show you how to put this thing to the test. The scientific method is this: when you find a possible clue to knowledge, you follow it out to see what there is in it. Now here is a possible clue to knowledge. Will you adopt the scientific method and follow it out to see what there is in it? Will you pray this prayer, 'O God, if there is any God, show me if Jesus Christ is Your Son or not, and if You show me that He is, I promise to accept Him as my Savior and confess Him as such before the world'?"

Very likely, here he would try to dodge again, but I would hold him to it. If he would not agree to this, I would show him that he was not an honest seeker after truth. If he agreed to do it, I would take him another step. I would have him turn to John 20:31, *"These are written* [the words contained in the gospel of John] *that you may believe that Jesus is the Christ, the Son of God, and that believing you may have life in His name."* Then I would say, "Now, here John presents the evidence that Jesus is the Son of God. Will you take the evidence and read it? Will you read the gospel of John?" Very likely, he would reply, "I have read it already." I would answer, "Yes, but I want you to read it in a new way. Read it slowly and thoughtfully, paying attention to what you read. I do not ask you to believe it; I do not ask you to try to believe it. I simply ask you to read it honestly, with a willingness to believe it if it is the truth. Each time, before you read, offer this prayer: 'O God, if there is any God, show me what truth there is in these verses I am about to read. I promise to commit myself to whatever You show me to be true.'"

If he refused to do this, I would show him he was not an honest seeker after the truth, that his unbelief was not his misfortune but his fault. If he agreed to do it, I would go over the three things he had agreed to do, and then say to him, "When you get through the gospel of John, will you report to me the result?" If I did not do this, he very likely would go away and not do what he had promised. I have never had anyone report to me that he had actually done the things I had asked him to do who did not arrive at faith in God, as well as in Jesus Christ as His Son and the Bible as His Word. I have tried this method with all kinds and conditions of men.

I also use another approach with inquirers. Sometimes, I immediately begin by showing a person that there is a God from the evidences of design in nature. I take out my watch and say, "Do you think this watch had an intelligent maker?" The inquirer replies, "Yes." I ask, "Why do you think it had an intelligent maker? Did you see the watch being made?" He answers, "No." "Did you ever see a watch being made?" He replies, "No." "Then why do you think it had an intelligent maker?" He will answer, "The watch shows the marks of intelligent design, thus proving it had an intelligent maker." Then I say to him, "What about your own eye? Is it not as wonderful a mechanism as a watch? Did it not then have a Maker?"

Everywhere in nature, we find symmetry, order, beauty, law, and utility. In the minutest forms of being that are discernible by the most powerful microscope, we see the same symmetry, order, beauty, law, and utility that are observable in the larger objects with which we are familiar. All this goes to prove the existence of an intelligent Creator and Designer of the physical universe.

The evolutionary hypothesis, even if it were true, would not take away any of the force of the argument from design in nature. For if it were true that the universe as we see it today, with all its countless forms of beauty and utility, came into being by a process of development from some primordial protoplasm, the question would at once arise, Who put into the primordial protoplasm the power to develop into the universe as we see it today?

From nature, then, we learn the existence of an intelligent, powerful, and benevolent Creator. Of course, nature does not teach us some of the more profound truths about God.

Q: What reasons do we have for being sure that God is a personal God—that He is a being with a personality and takes an active interest in our lives?

A: There are many conclusive proofs of the existence of a personal God. First, there is the proof from the evidence of design in nature, as referred to in the previous answer.

Second, history also proves the existence of a personal God. If we look at only a little patch of history, it sometimes seems as though there was no intelligent and benevolent purpose behind it. However, if we look at history in a large way, following its course through the centuries, we soon discover that behind the conflicting passions and ambitions of men, there is some intelligent and benevolent and righteous Power restraining and constraining man and causing the wrath of men to praise Him (Psalm 76:10).

We find in history that, as Matthew Arnold wrote, there is a "power, not ourselves, which makes for righteousness." From history we discover that there is a moral Governor of the universe. Everything in the universe is attuned to virtue. Everything in nature and history conspires to punish sin and reward virtue. This is a proof of the existence of a personal God.

Third, the history of Jesus of Nazareth, as recorded in the four Gospels, proves the existence of a personal God in a special way. It is one of the first principles of science that every effect must have an adequate cause, and the only cause that is adequate to account for the character, conduct, and works of Jesus of Nazareth is a God such as the Bible reveals. The attempt has been made, over and over again, and is still being made, to discount the miraculous in the history of Jesus of Nazareth. Indeed, the attempt is being made to eliminate the miracles altogether from that story, but every attempt of this kind has resulted in total failure. The ablest effort of this kind was made many years ago by David Strauss in his *Leben Jesu,* and for a while it seemed to a great many people as if David Strauss had succeeded. His theories were almost universally accepted in the universities of Europe. But his book could not bear careful critical examination and after a while was totally discredited. Every other attempt of the same kind has met with similar failure.

For any honest student of the New Testament today, this much at least is settled: the story of Jesus of Nazareth as recorded in the four Gospels is at least substantially accurate history. (To my mind, far more than this is proven, but that is enough for our present purpose.) If this is true—and it cannot be honestly denied by anyone who goes into the evidence—then the existence of a personal God is proven. Only a personal God will account for the life, character, conduct, and miracles of Jesus of Nazareth, and, above all, for His resurrection from the dead.

But the supreme proof of the existence of a personal God is found in the experience of the individual believer in Jesus Christ. Every real Christian knows God in personal experience. I know God more surely than I know any human being. I once doubted the existence of a personal God. I did not deny His existence; I simply questioned it. I was not an atheist, but I was an agnostic. However, I determined that if there were a God, I would know it. I became convinced from the study of history of the probability of the existence of God, but to me at that time, it was only a theory. I made up my mind to put to the test of rigid, personal experiment the theory that there was a God, and that the God of the Bible was the true God. I risked everything that men hold dear on this theory. If there had been no God, or if the God of the Bible had not been the true God, I would have lost everything that men hold dear years ago. But I risked, and I won, and today I know that there is a God and that the God of the Bible is the true God. Every other person may also know this by doing what I did.

There was a time in my life when I was put into a place where I literally lived by prayer to the God of the Bible, in the condition so clearly stated in the Bible. Every penny for my expenses came in answer to prayer. This included living expenses for myself and my wife and four children, rent for our home and for the halls in which I held meetings, support for missionaries, and funds for anything else that was needed. I made the commitment that I would not go into debt a cent for anything. When I could not pay, I would not buy. I gave up my salary, ceased taking collections or offerings, and told no one but God of any need. This went on for days and weeks and months. Every former source of income was cut off, and yet the money came— sometimes in very ordinary ways, sometimes in apparently most extraordinary ways, but it always came. When I was through, I knew that there is a personal God and that the God of the Bible is the true God. To me, God is the one great Reality who gives reality to all other realities.

Q: What do you mean by saying that God is a person? Does God have a body, or is He merely an invisible Spirit?

A: When we say that God is a person, we do not mean that He has hands and feet and legs and eyes and a nose. These are marks of bodily existence, not of personality. When we say that God is a person, we mean that He is a Being who knows and feels and wills and is not merely a blind, unintelligent force. Jesus said in John 4:24, *"God is* [a] *Spirit, and those who worship Him must worship in spirit and truth."* In Colossians 1:15, we read that God is *"invisible"* or unseeable.

But while God in His eternal essence is unseeable, He does manifest Himself in visible form. For example, we read in the ninth and tenth verses of Exodus 24 that Moses, Aaron, Nadab, Abihu, and seventy of the elders saw the God of Israel. It is also clear from a study of the different passages in the Old Testament where *"the Angel of the LORD"* is mentioned that it was God Himself who manifested Himself in this being. (See, for example, Genesis 16:7; Exodus 3:2.)

We are taught in Philippians 2:6 that Christ Jesus existed originally (*"being originally,"* RV, margin) *"in the form of God."* The Greek word translated *"form"* in this verse means the outward form, by which one is visible to the eye. Beyond a doubt, the thought here is that Jesus Christ, in His original state, was seen by the angelic world in a form that was outwardly manifested as divine. We may safely conclude, from this and other passages of Scripture, that while

God in His eternal essence is purely spiritual and invisible, He nevertheless manifests Himself in the angelic world and has manifested Himself from all eternity in an outward, visible form.

Q: What do you mean by "the Trinity"? How can God be one and three persons at the same time?

A: God cannot be one and three at the same time and in the same sense, and nowhere does the Bible teach that God is one and three in the same sense. Yet in what sense can He be one and three? A perfectly satisfactory answer to this question may be impossible from the very nature of the case. First, God is Spirit, and numbers belong primarily to the physical world. Difficulty inevitably arises when we attempt to describe the facts of spiritual being in the forms of physical expression. Second, God is infinite, and we are finite. Our attempts at a philosophical explanation of the triunity of God is an attempt to put the facts of infinite being into the forms of finite thought. Such an attempt, at the very best, can only be partially successful. The doctrine of the Trinity, which has been the accepted doctrine of the church through so many centuries, is the most successful attempt in that direction, but it may be questioned whether it is a full and final statement of the truth.

This much we know, that God is essentially one. We also know that there are three persons who possess the attributes of deity—the Father, the Son, and the Holy Spirit—who are called God and who are to be worshipped as God. There is only one God, but this one God makes Himself known to us as Father, Son, and Holy Spirit. Yet the Son and the Spirit are both subordinate to the Father. God the Father is God in the absolute and final sense—God in the source. The Son is God in the outflow. All the perfections of a fountain are in the river that flows forth from the fountain. Similarly, the Father has imparted to the Son all His own perfections, so that it may be said without qualification that *"he who has seen* [the Son] *has seen the Father"* (John 14:9). Through all eternity, the Son has existed and has possessed all the perfections of the Father. While He possesses all the perfections of the Father, He is not the Father but is derived from the Father and is eternally subordinate to the Father. This seems to be as far as we can go in our understanding now. How much further we may go in that glad, coming day when we will no longer see *"through a glass, darkly; but...face to face"* (1 Corinthians 13:12 KJV), when we will no longer *"know in part"* (v. 12) but will know God as perfectly and as thoroughly as He now knows us, none of us can tell.

Q: If God is a God of mercy and love, and if He is the Director of the universe, why does He send earthquakes, tidal waves, and other phenomena when thousands of lives are lost almost instantly through them?

A: Because He sees fit to do so. If God saw fit, He would have a perfect right to plunge the whole earth beneath a flood and leave us all to perish instantly. All men have sinned. All men deserve the wrath of God. But God loves even a sinful and apostate race, and He has provided a way of pardon for all who will accept it—and not only a way of pardon but also a way by which we may become sons of God and heirs of God and joint heirs with Jesus Christ. (See John 1:12; Romans 8:14–17.) If anyone who accepts this way of pardon is swept away by an earthquake, tidal wave, or other disaster, he loses nothing. He departs to *"be with Christ, which is far better"* (Philippians 1:23). If anyone does not accept this way of pardon, he is utterly wicked and ungrateful. His being swept away by an earthquake, tidal wave, or other phenomenon is far less than he deserves and far less than he will receive in the Judgment that awaits him in the world to come—not merely for his sins but also for the black ingratitude of his trampling underfoot the mercy of God that has been so marvelously manifested (Hebrews 10:29).

In our day, men have largely forgotten that God is God, and they think that He is under an obligation to explain His dealings to us. God's ways are not our ways, and God's thoughts are not our thoughts. But as the heavens are higher than the earth, so are His ways higher than our ways, and His thoughts than our thoughts (Isaiah 55:8–9). His judgments are unsearchable, and His ways are beyond finding out (Romans 11:33). But when we reach the other side and no longer *"see through a glass, darkly; but...face to face"* (1 Corinthians 13:12 KJV), then we will understand that the providences of God that were the most difficult for us to comprehend in this present life were full of mercy and kindness to man. What we all need to learn now is that God, in His infinite wisdom, may have a thousand good reasons for doing something when we, in our finite ignorance, cannot see even one reason for it.

Q: If God exercises general governance and control over the entire universe, how do you explain the apparent dominance of sin?

A: It is only on this earth that sin is apparently dominant, and this earth is a very small portion of the universe. Furthermore, God's plans are eternal and will take eternity for their full working out. The apparent dominance of sin is only temporary. Through permitting it at the present time, God is working out His own plans of good. When these plans are worked out, we will see how the controlling power of God was all the time behind man's failures, rebellions, and sin. Indeed, we can see it to a large degree even at the present time.

GOOD WORKS

Q: May I merit heaven by my good works?

A: If your works are absolutely perfect, if you never break the law of God at any point from the hour of your birth until your death, if you do all that God requires of you and all that pleases Him, you can merit heaven by your good works. But this is something that no man except Jesus Christ has ever done or can ever do. *"There is no difference; for all have sinned and fall short of the glory of God"* (Romans 3:22–23). The moment any person breaks the law of God at any point, he can no longer merit heaven by his good works. The law demands perfect obedience (Galatians 3:10). Nothing but perfect obedience to the law of God will secure life or heaven. There is, therefore, no hope on the basis of our own works.

The moment a person has sinned at any point, his only hope is that he be justified freely through the grace of God in Jesus Christ (Romans 3:24). But justification by free grace is offered to all who will accept Jesus Christ. All who believe are *"justified freely"*—that is, as a free gift—*"through the redemption that is in Christ Jesus"* (v. 24). God set Him forth to be the *"propitiation* [atoning sacrifice] *by His blood, through faith"* (v. 25). If you will study the whole passage, starting from the ninth verse of Romans 3 and reading through the eighth verse of Romans 4, you will see how impossible it is for anyone to merit heaven by his good works, and what God's method of justification is.

GUARDIAN ANGELS

Q: Please explain Matthew 18:10: *"Take heed that you do not despise one of these little ones, for I say to you that in heaven their angels always see the face of My Father who is in heaven."* Does every child have a guardian angel?

A: This seems to be the plain teaching of the text. Some explain the text in another way. They say that the angels of the children that are spoken of here are the departed spirits of the children in the glory. However, there is not a hint anywhere in the Bible that the departed spirits of human beings are angels. All through the Bible, the clearest distinction is kept between angels and men. The old hymn, "I Want to Be an Angel," has no warrant whatsoever in Scripture.

The angels of the children that are spoken of here are the angels who watch over the children. It is the office of angels to minister on behalf of those who will be heirs of salvation (Hebrews 1:14). According to the Bible, each child seems to have a guardian angel, and these angels occupy a position of special favor and opportunity before God. They stand in His very presence and always behold the face of the Father.

106

THE HEATHEN

Q: How is God going to judge the heathen? Can the heathen be saved by following the best spiritual light they have?

A: God will judge the heathen in righteousness, according to the light they have had. Those who have sinned without knowing the law revealed to Moses will also perish without the law, and those who have sinned under the law will be judged by the law (Romans 2:12).

The heathen are not without spiritual light. The fact that they do by nature the things required in the law shows that they have a law, though not the law revealed to Moses (Romans 2:14–16). If any heathen were to perfectly live up to the light he has, he would undoubtedly be saved by doing so, but no heathen has ever done this. The twelfth through sixteenth verses of Romans 2 are often taken as teaching that the heathen are to be saved by the light of nature. However, anyone who will read the passage carefully in its context will see that Paul's whole purpose was not to show how the heathen are saved by keeping the law written in their hearts but to show that all are under condemnation—the Jew because he has not lived up to the law given by revelation, and the Gentile because he has not lived up to the law written in his heart. The conclusion of the matter is given in Romans 3:22–23: *"For there is no difference; for all have sinned and fall short of the glory of God."*

The verses that follow this passage point out the only way of salvation: free justification by God's grace through the redemption that is in Christ Jesus on the basis of His atoning death. Each person secures for himself this justification by faith in Christ (vv. 24–25). No one will be saved except through personal acceptance of Jesus Christ as his personal Savior. There is not a line of Scripture that holds out a ray of hope to anyone who dies without accepting Jesus Christ.

There are those who believe that people who die without hearing of Jesus Christ in this world will have an opportunity to hear of Him and to accept or reject Him in some future state. However, the Bible does not say so; this is pure speculation without a word of Scripture to support it. There are also those who believe that the heathen who would have accepted Christ if He had been presented to them will be treated as if He had been presented to them and they had accepted Him, but this is all pure speculation.

All that the Bible teaches is that no one can be saved without personal acceptance of Christ, and it is wisdom on our part to do everything in our power to see that the heathen have the opportunity to accept Christ in this present life. We do not have one word of Scripture to support us in the hope that if we neglect our duty here, the heathen will have an opportunity to accept Christ in some future age or state.

HEAVEN

Q: Is heaven a place or a state of the soul?

A: Jesus Christ plainly declared that heaven is a place. In John 14:2, He said, *"I go to prepare a place for you."* To make it even plainer, He added in the next verse that when the place is prepared, He will come again and receive us to Himself, so that *where* He is, we may be also (v. 3). Furthermore, we are distinctly told that when Jesus Himself left this earth, He went into heaven, from where He had come. (See, for example, John 13:3; Acts 1:9–11; Ephesians 1:20–21.)

The blessedness of heaven will not all be due to the character of the place. It will be even more blessed because of the state of mind that those who inhabit heaven will be in. Nevertheless, heaven is a place, a place more beautiful than any of us can imagine. All earthly comparisons necessarily fail. In our present state, every sense and faculty of perception is blunted by sin and by the disease that results from sin. In our redeemed bodies, every sense and faculty will be enlarged and will exist in perfection. There may be new senses, but what they may be, we cannot of course now imagine. The most beautiful sights that we have ever seen on earth are nothing compared with what will greet us in that fair *"city which has foundations"* (Hebrews 11:10). Heaven will be free from everything that curses or mars our lives here. There will be no menial, grinding toil, no sickness or pain, no death, no funerals, and no separations. (See Revelation 21:4; 1 Thessalonians 4:13–17.) Above all, there will be no sin. It will be a place of universal and perfect knowledge, universal and perfect love, and perpetual praise. (See 1 Corinthians 13:12; 1 John 3:2; 4:8; Revelation 7:9–12.) It will be a land of melody and song.

Q: What must one do to get to heaven?

A: To get to heaven, a person needs to accept Jesus Christ as his personal Savior, surrender to Him as his Lord and Master, and openly confess Him as such before the world. Jesus Christ said, *"I am the way, the truth, and the life. No one comes to the Father except through Me"* (John 14:6). He also said, *"I am the door. If anyone enters by Me, he will be saved"* (John 10:9). When a person receives Jesus, he immediately becomes a child of God, an heir of God, and a joint heir with Jesus Christ (John 1:12; Romans 8:16–17).

Anyone can know whether or not he is already on the way to heaven by simply asking himself these questions: "Have I received Jesus Christ? Have I taken Him as my Sin-Bearer, the One who bore my sins in His own body on the cross? (See Isaiah 53:6; 1 Peter 2:24; Galatians 3:13.) Am I trusting God to forgive my sins because Jesus Christ bore them for me? Have I taken Jesus Christ as my Lord and Master? Have I surrendered my mind to Him so that it may be renewed by Him, and my life to Him so that He may guide me in everything? Am I confessing Him as my Savior and my Lord before the world as I have opportunity?"

If anyone can answer yes to these simple questions, he may know he is on the way to heaven. Of course, if one has really received Jesus as his Lord and Master, he will prove it by studying His Word day by day in order to know His will, and by doing His will as he finds it revealed in the Bible.

Q: Is the Bible an all-sufficient guide to heaven?

A: It is. It tells each one of us what sort of a place heaven is and just how to get there. There is not a thing a person needs to know about the road to heaven that is not plainly stated in the Bible. It is the only Book in the world that reveals Jesus Christ, and Jesus Christ Himself is the way to heaven (John 14:6).

Q: Will we recognize our loved ones in heaven?

A: Most assuredly, we will. The apostle Paul, in writing to the believers of Thessalonica, told them not to sorrow over their loved ones, from whom they would be separated for a time, as those who have no hope sorrow over the loss of their loved ones (1 Thessalonians 4:13). He went on to say that Jesus Himself is coming back again and that our loved ones who have fallen asleep in Jesus will be raised first. Then we who are alive will be transformed and caught up together with them to meet the Lord in the air (vv. 14–18). The whole reason for this exhortation was to let the believers know that when we are caught up together with our loved ones, we will be with them again. Furthermore, Moses and Elijah appeared to the three disciples who were with Christ on the Mount of Transfiguration, and were recognized by them. (See Matthew 17:1–4.) If we will recognize those whom we have never known in the flesh, how much more will we recognize our loved ones!

Q: Can a person be happy in heaven if he knows his loved ones are in hell?

A: Yes. A real Christian's supreme joy is in Jesus Christ (Matthew 10:37). The love that he has for even the dearest of his earthly loved ones is nothing compared with the love that he has for Jesus Christ, and Jesus Christ is in heaven. Jesus will satisfy every longing of the heart that really knows Him.

Furthermore, if any of our loved ones end up in hell, they will be there simply because they persistently rejected and trampled underfoot that

One who is the supreme object of our love (Hebrews 10:29). They will be with the Devil and his angels because they chose to cast in their lot with them, and we will recognize the justice of it and the necessity of it. Many people will not allow themselves to believe in eternal punishment because they have unrepentant friends and loved ones. However, it is far better to recognize the facts, no matter how unwelcome they may be, and to try to save our loved ones from the doom to which they are certainly hurrying, than it is to quarrel with facts and seek to remove them by shutting our eyes to them. If we love Jesus Christ supremely, if we love Him as we should love Him, and if we realize His glory and His claims upon men as we should realize them, we will say, if the dearest friend we have on earth persists in trampling Christ underfoot, that he ought to be tormented forever. If, after men have sinned and merited God's terrible wrath, God still offers them mercy and makes the tremendous sacrifice of His Son to save them, and if, after all this, they still despise that mercy, trample God's Son underfoot, and are consigned to everlasting torment, anyone who sees as he ought to see will say, "Amen. True and righteous are Your judgments, O Lord!" (See Revelation 16:7.)

HELL

Q: Is hell a place or a state of the soul?

A: Hell, meaning the final abode of Satan and the unrepentant, is plainly declared in the Bible to be a place prepared for the Devil and his angels. For a more thorough discussion of this topic and supporting Scripture passages, please refer to the following sections in this book: "The Devil," "Eternal Punishment," and "Heaven."

Q: Please explain Psalm 139:8: *"If I ascend into heaven, You are there; if I make my bed in hell, behold, You are there."* I cannot imagine God's presence in hell.

A: The word translated *"hell"* in this passage does not mean hell in the sense of the abode of the lost. It means the place where all the dead were before our Lord's ascension. (It is rendered as *"Sheol"* in the New American Standard Bible and the Revised Version. This is not a translation. It is the actual Hebrew word used.) Both the righteous and unrighteous dead went to sheol—the righteous to that portion of sheol known as paradise, and the unrighteous to the place of suffering. Since God is everywhere, He must in some sense be present even in hell, but He certainly does not manifest His presence there as He does in heaven, or even as He does on earth.

THE HOLY SPIRIT

Q: Does the Holy Spirit live in and remain with the believer, or does He come and go?

A: I know of no place in the Bible where it is recorded that He comes and goes from the believer. It is true that the Spirit of the Lord departed from King Saul (1 Samuel 16:14), but we have no reason to believe that Saul was a true believer, a regenerate man. The Holy Spirit dwells in the believer, according to the teaching of Jesus Christ (John 14:17). The believer may grieve Him (Ephesians 4:30), but the Bible does not say that the believer "grieves Him away," as it is sometimes quoted as saying. Indeed, it distinctly says that even though we grieve Him, we are *sealed for the day of redemption*" (v. 30). The believer, through sin or worldliness, may lose the consciousness of the indwelling presence of the Spirit of God. However, losing the consciousness of His presence and power is one thing; actually losing His presence is another. The Holy Spirit may withdraw into the innermost sanctuary of the believer's spirit, behind the believer's conscious awareness of His indwelling, but He is still there.

There is, however, a work of the Holy Spirit upon a person that is short of regeneration, as in conviction. In such a case, He may come and go.

Q: Please discuss waiting on God for power for service.

A: Our Lord Jesus distinctly taught in Acts 1:8 that there is a definite endowment of power from the

Holy Spirit for those who seek it. The experience of thousands of ministers and other believers proves the same. This power is received under the following conditions:

♦ First, that we rest absolutely on the finished work of Christ as the only basis for our acceptance before God.

♦ Second, that we put out of our lives every known sin.

♦ Third, that we surrender absolutely to God for Him to use us as He wills.

♦ Fourth, that we openly confess our acceptance of Jesus Christ as our Savior and Lord before the world.

♦ Fifth, that we really desire this anointing.

♦ Sixth, that we definitely ask for it.

♦ Seventh, that we take by faith what we ask for. (See Mark 11:24; 1 John 5:14–15.)

There does not need to be a long time of waiting. God is ready to give the Holy Spirit at once (Luke 11:13). Of course, waiting on God is something that every believer should practice. Undoubtedly, God gives His Spirit when people individually or together spend a long time in prayer before Him, thus recognizing and acknowledging their dependence upon Him. However, the teaching that a person may have to wait a month or six months for "his Pentecost" has no foundation in the Bible.

IMMORTALITY

Q: How do you prove the immortality of the soul?

A: In the Bible, immortality as applied to man is used of the body and not of the soul, but I suppose the question means: How do you prove that there is a future existence after death?

We prove it from the Bible. In another of my books, I have proven that the Bible is the Word of God and that all its teachings are absolutely reliable.* The Bible teaches beyond a doubt that all men will be raised from the dead—the righteous to the resurrection of life, and those who have done evil to the resurrection of judgment (John 5:28–29). It furthermore teaches what the exact state of those who accept Christ and of those who reject Christ will be in the future eternal existence. (See also the sections on "Eternal Punishment" and "Heaven" in this book.) Moreover, the resurrection of Jesus Christ is one of the best-proven facts of history and demonstrably proves that death is not the end of everything.

There are scientific and philosophical arguments for immortality, but if we leave out the arguments that are built on the resurrection of Jesus

---

*See R. A. Torrey, *Powerful Faith* (New Kensington, PA: Whitaker House, 1996).

117

Christ, all that these other arguments prove is the probability of life after death, the probability of a future existence. However, when we include the arguments based on the Bible—above all, the resurrection of Jesus Christ—our belief in a future existence is no longer based on a mere probability. It is removed from the domain of the merely probable into the domain of the absolutely certain and proven.

Q: Do the Scriptures teach conditional immortality?

A: The doctrine of conditional immortality is that man is naturally mortal and only gains immortality in Christ. There is an element of truth in the belief that man is naturally mortal. Since man began to exist at one point, he could, of course, cease to exist. But it is the plain teaching of Scripture that all the sons of Adam receive endless existence through Christ. In 1 Corinthians 15:22, we are told that *"as in Adam all die, even so in Christ all shall be made alive."* If we deal fairly with these words, one *"all"* is as comprehensive as the other. Everyone who loses existence in Adam, who returns to the dust (Genesis 3:19; 5:5), is raised from the dust in Christ. The whole race gets back in Christ what it lost in Adam.

But whether this existence, this immortality that we receive in Christ, will be a resurrection to life or a resurrection to judgment and everlasting shame and contempt (John 5:28–29; Daniel 12:2) depends entirely on what we do with the Christ in whom we receive it. Every man's endless existence becomes an existence of unspeakable blessedness if he accepts Christ, but that existence becomes an existence of unspeakable misery if he rejects Christ. It is *"the second death"* (Revelation 21:8), a share with the Devil and his angels in the lake of fire prepared for them (Matthew 25:41), a portion in the lake of fire where there is no rest, day or night, forever and ever (Revelation 20:10).

INFANTS

Q: Are those who die in infancy lost forever?

A: There is not a line of Scripture to indicate that they are. Jesus said, *"Let the little children come to Me, and do not forbid them; for of such is the kingdom of heaven"* (Matthew 19:14). It is true that infants are born into this world as members of a fallen race under the condemnation of God, that Adam's sin is imputed to all his descendants, but the sins of the whole race were atoned for by the death of Jesus Christ on the cross. (See 1 Timothy 2:6; John 1:29; 1 Corinthians 15:22; 1 John 2:2.) This includes the children.

When a child reaches the age of accountability and commits sin, there must be a definite personal acceptance of Christ before he can be saved, but of course this does not apply to those who die in infancy. To them, Christ's *"one act of righteousness"* (Romans 5:18 NIV)—His atoning death on the cross—brings the free gift of *"justification that brings life"* (v. 18 NIV). The time will come when these children will see Christ and believe in Him, and thus be saved in the fullest sense. They will never perish for Adam's sin. Jesus Christ bore the penalty of Adam's sin for them. No one is lost merely because of Adam's sin. There is absolutely no basis in Scripture for the doctrine of the damnation of infants.

Q: Is there any Scripture that demonstrates that the children of unbelieving parents will be saved if they die in infancy? If so, what does the latter part of 1 Corinthians 7:14 mean: *"The unbelieving husband is sanctified by the wife, and the unbelieving wife is sanctified by the husband; otherwise your children would be unclean, but now they are holy"*?

A: The latter part of this verse undoubtedly teaches that the children of believing parents stand in a different relation to God than the children of unbelieving parents. However, there is no teaching anywhere in the Bible that an infant who dies is eternally lost, as explained in the preceding answer.

Q: Where do those who die in their infancy go in the other world?

A: The Bible does not tell us specifically. It does, however, say that *"of such is the kingdom of heaven"* (Matthew 19:14). There is absolutely no basis in Scripture for the doctrine that while infants do not go to the place of torment, they go to a place where there is not that fullness of blessedness that those who live to maturity and accept Jesus Christ enter into. We are not wise to go beyond what is written and make theories of our own regarding their future destiny, but certainly there is not the slightest ground for any anxiety regarding them.

INSURANCE

Q: Some people maintain that Christians should not insure their lives, property, etc., because by so doing they are distrusting God and His providential care. What does the Bible teach regarding this?

A: The Bible teaches that there is no conflict between trusting God and an intelligent and wise provision for the necessities of the future. For instance, we read in Proverbs 6:6–8: *"Go to the ant, you sluggard! Consider her ways and be wise, which, having no captain, overseer or ruler, provides her supplies in the summer, and gathers her food in the harvest."* Let's consider another biblical example. The apostle Paul had been imprisoned and was being taken on a ship to Rome by way of Crete. A great storm arose, and it looked as if everyone on the ship would be lost. But Paul prayed, and he received God's own assurance that both he and all those who were with him on the ship would be saved. He fully believed God that it would come out just as he had been told. Nevertheless, when the sailors tried to flee out of the ship, thus imperiling the vessel, Paul saw to it that they were not allowed to escape. (See Acts 27:21–36.) This was not an act of unbelief on Paul's part. He was simply cooperating with God in the fulfillment of His promise.

Now, as to whether it is an intelligent and wise provision for the future to insure one's life or to insure one's property, is another question that each one must decide prayerfully for himself. God promises wisdom to each one of us in the settling of such questions, if we look to Him for it and meet the conditions of answered prayer (James 1:5–8). But even if it proved to be an unwise expenditure of money to insure one's life or property, that still would not make it an act of distrust in God.

THE JEWS

Q: Is there any difference today in God's sight between Jews and Gentiles?

A: Most assuredly, there is. In 1 Corinthians 10:32, the apostle Paul divided men into three categories: the Jews, the Gentiles, and the church of

God. Today, God has His plans for the Jew, His plans for the Gentile, and His plans for the church.

In the church, there is neither Jew nor Gentile (Galatians 3:28). When one accepts Jesus Christ as his Savior, surrenders to Him as his Lord and Master, and openly confesses Him as such before the world, he becomes part of the body of Christ, that is, part of the church. The relationship of the Jewish Christian to Christ is precisely the same as that of the Gentile Christian. The promises that belong to one belong to the other; the Scriptures that belong to one belong to the other. The method of dividing the Word that some employ, applying some of the promises to Jewish Christians and others to Gentile Christians, is not warranted by the Word. What belongs to any Christian belongs to all Christians, both Jewish and Gentile.

But outside of the church, there is Jew and Gentile, and God's plans are not precisely the same for both. The present dispensation is preeminently a Gentile dispensation. The Jew, for the time being, has been set aside, but his day is coming. (See, for example, Romans 11:1–32.)

JUDGMENT

Q: Do the Scriptures teach that there will be one general judgment or several judgments?

A: The Scriptures plainly teach that there will be several judgments. There will be, first of all, the judgment of the believer when he is caught up to meet the Lord in the air. This will not be a judgment regarding his salvation—for that is settled the moment he accepts Christ (John 5:24)—but a judgment regarding his reward (1 Corinthians 3:13–15; 2 Timothy 4:8). Then there will be the judgment of the nations living on this earth at the time the Lord comes to earth with His saints, described in Matthew 25:31–46. But those who do not have a part in the first resurrection will not be raised for their judgment for a thousand years (Revelation 20:4–5). At the end of the thousand years, the Millennium, the rest of the dead will be raised and will appear before God at the judgment of the Great White Throne (vv. 11–15).

Q: Does God soften the final judgment of those who sin ignorantly?

A: Certainly, God does not deal with those who sin ignorantly as He does with those who sin by deliberate and willful choice. (See 1 Timothy 1:13; compare Hebrews 10:26.) But every person on this earth has sinned knowingly (Romans 3:10–12, 23), and therefore there is no hope for anyone outside the atoning work of Jesus Christ (vv. 24–26). Everyone who believes in Jesus Christ receives eternal life, and all who reject Him will not see life but will perish forever (John 3:36; 2 Thessalonians 1:7–10).

MAN IN GOD'S IMAGE

Q: What does Genesis 1:27 mean when it says that *"God created man in His own image"*?

A: We are told in Colossians 3:10 that the regenerated man is *"renewed in knowledge according to the image of Him who created him."* In Ephesians 4:24, we are told that it is in *"true righteousness and holiness"* that the *"new man"* is created in the image of God. It is evident, then, that the words *"image"* and *"likeness"* in Genesis 1:26–27 do not refer to visible or bodily likeness but to intellectual and moral likeness in *"knowledge"* and *"true righteousness and holiness."* However, we are taught in Philippians 2:6 that Christ Jesus existed originally (*"being originally,"* RV, margin) *"in the form of God"*—that is, in a visible form that was divine. Similarly, in our ultimate state of blessedness, we will be like Christ in our bodily appearance as well as intellectually and morally. (See 1 John 3:2; compare Matthew 13:43 with Matthew 17:2.)

MARRIAGE

Q: Should a Christian ever marry an unbeliever?

A: Most assuredly not. To do so is to disobey the plainest directions of God's Word. God says in 2 Corinthians 6:14, *"Do not be unequally yoked together with unbelievers."* Undoubtedly, many do this through ignorance, but that does not make it right. When a woman and a man marry, they are yoked together in the most complete and intimate sense. By *"unbelievers"* in the above passage, God clearly does not merely mean outright "pagans," but all who have not definitely received Jesus Christ and surrendered their lives to Him.

More promising lives are shipwrecked by a marriage contrary to the Word of God than in almost any other way. Some women marry men for the purpose of converting them. Such marriages result in inevitable and unutterable misery. You cannot hope to convert another by disobeying God yourself.

Q: Do you believe in marriages between Catholics and Protestants?

A: While both Roman Catholics and Protestants may be real believers in the Lord Jesus Christ, the differences between them are so radical that a marriage between the two cannot but result in friction and misunderstanding. This will especially be true when children are born into the family and the question of rearing the children comes up. If the two parties in question cannot come to see eye to eye on the fundamental questions of difference between Catholics and Protestants before their marriage, then they had better not marry.

Q: Is the marriage of cousins sanctioned in the Bible?

A: There is no explicit commandment in the Bible that cousins should not marry, but it is a well-known fact that the marriage of near relatives is fraught with great physical dangers. If there is any hereditary taint in the family, it will be accentuated in the children of near relatives. For example, in countries where there has been constant intermarriage of relatives, many of the children are mentally disabled and have other genetic defects. Certainly, the Bible does not sanction two people entering into a marriage when the children would potentially be at such great risk.

MEDICINE

Q: James 5:14–15 says, *"Is anyone among you sick? Let him call for the elders of the church, and let them pray over him, anointing him with oil in the name of the Lord. And the prayer of faith will save the sick, and the Lord will raise him up."* Does this passage give grounds for believing that medical aid should have no place in the life of faith, or does the Lord expect us to use the means at hand, praying for His blessing upon such means?

A: This passage does not give grounds for believing that medical aid should never have any place in the life of faith. It tells us what we should do when we are sick, but it says nothing either for or against medicine. Undoubtedly, it is often the purpose of God to heal without any means except those mentioned in this passage, but it is also plainly taught in the Word of God that the use of medicinal means may be proper, as in 1 Timothy 5:23: *"No longer drink only water, but use a little wine for your stomach's sake and your frequent infirmities."*

THE MILLENNIUM

Q: What is the Millennium?

A: *Millennium* means one thousand years, and the Millennium is the thousand-year reign of Christ on earth after His second coming (Revelation 20:4, 6). There are many prophecies about Christ as an earthly King that have not yet been fulfilled but that will be fulfilled in His millennial reign on earth. He will occupy the throne of David. (See Jeremiah 23:5–6; Psalm 2:6; Zechariah 14:9.) This does not mean that He will sit on a throne in Jerusalem all the time. The king of a country occupies its throne, but he very seldom literally sits upon that throne. It may be that, much of the time, Christ will be with His bride in the New Jerusalem, and not in the old literal Jerusalem here on earth, but He will reign as King on earth for one thousand years.

Q: Will the Millennium be a period of soul-saving revival?

A: There seems to be reason to suppose that, in connection with the return of our Lord, the events that accompany it will result in many people coming to their senses and to an acceptance of Jesus Christ. Certainly, this is true of Israel. There is to be a national repentance, a national turning to Christ. Jesus, coming as a Deliverer, *"will turn away ungodliness from Jacob"* (Romans 11:26). God will pour out upon Israel *"the Spirit of grace and supplication"* (Zechariah 12:10). They will look upon the One whom they have pierced, and they will mourn over their sin. A fountain will be opened to them so that they may be cleansed from sin and uncleanness, and there will be a national turning to Jesus Christ. (See Zechariah 12:10–13:1.)

In connection with the conversion of Israel, there will also be a great turning of the Gentiles to Christ. *"Because of [Israel's] transgression, salvation has come to the Gentiles to make Israel envious. But if their transgression means riches for the world, and their loss means riches for the Gentiles, how much greater riches will their fullness bring!"* (Romans 11:11–12 NIV).

MIRACLES

Q: How are miracles possible if the laws of nature are fixed?

A: God is the Author of the laws of nature. The laws of nature indicate God's customary ways of working. To what extent they are fixed, it is impossible to say. But even if they were absolutely fixed, that would not make miracles impossible. One of the most universally recognized laws of nature is the law of gravity. According to the law of gravity, a stone lying on the surface of the earth will be drawn toward the center of the earth. However, it is quite possible for a man to come along and, if he wills to do so, to lift that stone away from the earth. The law of gravity is not violated in the least, but a higher law, the law of the human will, steps in and produces an effect just the opposite of what the law of gravity by itself would have produced. If a human being can bring things to pass that the fixed law of nature would not have brought to pass, left to itself, how much more can a mighty God who is the Creator of all things do so!

This whole argument about miracles being impossible because of the fixed laws of nature appears wise to the shallow thinker, but when we look right at it, it is found to be supremely absurd. The real question is not whether miracles are possible, but rather if they have occurred and if they are well attested. Miracles are certainly well attested. The supreme miracle of all is the resurrection of Jesus Christ from the dead. A leading agnostic has said, "We do not need to discuss the other miracles. The whole question is, Did Jesus Christ rise from the dead? If He did, it is easy enough to believe the other miracles. If He did not, the miraculous must go." He has stated the case well. If Jesus Christ did rise from the dead, then the miraculous is proven. The argument for the resurrection of Jesus Christ from the dead is simply overwhelming. The resurrection of Jesus Christ from the dead is one of the best-proven facts of history.* Therefore, it is plain that miracles are not only possible but also historically certain.

Q: Has the age of miracles passed away? Why doesn't God work miracles today as in Christ's time?

A: There is no conclusive biblical proof that God does not work miracles today, nor is there any proof in history or experience. That physical miracles are not as frequent and abundant as they were when Jesus Christ Himself was on the earth is only to be expected. When Jesus was on the earth, He was God manifested in the flesh; but now He is with us in the Spirit, and the miracles that we should

---

*For a discussion of the evidence for the Resurrection, see R. A. Torrey, *Powerful Faith* (New Kensington, PA: Whitaker House, 1996).

expect to see more abundantly in the present time are in the spiritual realm. Regeneration is a miracle. The raising of a spirit dead in trespasses and sins to life in Jesus Christ is a more wonderful miracle than the resurrection of the body. This miracle is constantly occurring. In fact, those who believe in Jesus Christ today are doing greater things in the spiritual realm than Jesus Christ accomplished while He was here on earth. This is only the fulfillment of Christ's own words (John 14:12).

We may expect that physical miracles will be more common again when Christ returns the second time to reign on earth.

MISSIONS

Q: What part should support for missions have in the life of the church and the individual believer?

A: A very prominent part. Our Lord's last command to His disciples was, *"Go therefore and make disciples of all the nations"* (Matthew 28:19). It was in connection with this work that He promised His own personal fellowship. He said that when we do this, *"Lo, I am with you always, even to the end of the age"* (v. 20). If, then, the individual believer wishes to have personal fellowship with Jesus Christ, he must go into all the world and *"make disciples of all the nations."* He may not be able to go personally, but in that case, he can go by his gifts and by his prayers. Any Christian who is not deeply interested in missions is not in fellowship with Jesus Christ.

Since a true church is a fellowship of obedient believers, what is true of each believer will be true of the church, with the added power and blessing that comes from cooperation.

THE OLD TESTAMENT LAW

Q: Should Christians keep the Law of Moses? Is a Christian under law?

A: No. We are taught in Galatians 5:18, *"If you are led by the Spirit, you are not under the law."* But this does not mean for a moment that a Christian is to lead a lawless life. While we are not under the Law of Moses, we are under law to Christ; that is, we are under obligation to do, in all things, what pleases our new Husband, Christ. (See Romans 7:1–4.) Those who are led by the Spirit—who are the only ones who are not under law—will not do things that are forbidden by the Spirit in the Word of God.

There are many in our day who have gone into the most foolish extravagances in regard to not being under the law. They say that they are led by the

Spirit and therefore are not under any obligation to obey the Word. They do things that they say the Spirit leads them to do that are directly contrary to the will of God as revealed in the Bible. Now, the Bible is the Holy Spirit's Book, and the Holy Spirit certainly does not lead a person to do things that are contrary to the Bible. Any spirit that leads men to do things that are contrary to the teachings of the Bible is certainly not the Holy Spirit. There are some Christians, for instance, who scoff at all obligation to keep the Lord's Day differently from other days, and who ridicule as being under the law those who do set this day apart. These people are unscriptural and are doing much harm. While they claim to be in subjection to the Holy Spirit, they are really in subjection only to their own headstrong self-will and spiritual pride.

ORIGINAL SIN

Q: What is original sin, and why is it just to hold us guilty of it?

A: The phrase *original sin* is used nowadays in a great variety of senses and is generally used inaccurately. Strictly speaking, original sin was the sin in which all other sins originated, that is, the sin of Adam and Eve in the Garden of Eden.

It is just to hold us guilty for this sin, first, because we were all in Adam when he committed the sin, and second, because Adam, who was the whole race as it existed at that time, sinned as our representative, and we sinned in him (Romans 5:12; 1 Corinthians 15:21–22). But when Jesus came as the Second Adam, He also was our Representative, the Representative of the whole race, the Son of Man. When He perfectly kept the law of God, He kept it as our Representative. By His atoning death, He cleared us from the guilt of the sin committed in Adam (Romans 5:15–18). No one will be lost because of Adam's sin. If anyone is lost, it will simply be because he did not accept the Second Adam.

God's plan of holding us guilty because of Adam's sin is much more merciful than if each of us had had to stand for himself. If each of us had stood for himself, we would all have done just what Adam did. We would have sinned, and there would have been no hope. But because the first Adam stood as our representative, the Second Adam could also stand as our Representative. He did for us what not one of us would have done for ourselves. He perfectly kept the law of God, and, having perfectly kept it, He died for us who had broken it—not only broken it in Adam's sin but also broken it in our own personal transgression. There is a depth of mercy as well as wisdom in God's plan that will fill us with wonder and praise throughout all eternity!

PERFECTION

Q: Can a person live a faultless life?

A: No one lives a faultless life, and no one can live a faultless life unless he is perfect in knowledge. The sincerest men and women may make mistakes in moral judgment. We are constantly growing in our knowledge of God's will as we study His Word. If, at any point, we fall below God's highest will, our lives are not faultless.

However, while we cannot live a faultless life, we can live a *blameless* life; that is, we can live up to our highest understanding of God's will as revealed in His Word. We are not to blame for what we do not know, except when our lack of knowledge is the result of our own neglect. (See Colossians 1:21–23; 1 Thessalonians 2:10; 3:13; 5:23.) Every child of God should aim to lead a blameless life, but those who lead the most blameless lives are the most conscious of their deficiencies and know how far their lives are from being absolutely faultless.

Q: Is the doctrine of sinless perfection scriptural? How can the sixth and ninth verses of 1 John 3 and related passages in that epistle be adequately reconciled with the eighth and tenth verses of 1 John 1?

A: They can be adequately reconciled by noticing exactly what John said. In 1 John 3:6, he said,

"Whoever abides in [Christ] *does not sin."* The phrase *"does not sin"* literally means "is not sinning," that is, is not practicing sin. The verb is in the present tense, which denotes continuous present action. John did not say that the believer never sins, but that he does not make a practice of sinning, does not continue sinning. This is the exact force of the language used here. The same thing may be said of 1 John 3:9. The literal translation of the words of this verse is, "Every one begotten out of God is not doing sin (that is, sin is not his practice), because His seed (that is, God's seed) abides in him, and he cannot be sinning (be making a practice of sin) because he is begotten out of God."

We should also bear in mind John's definition of sin in the fourth verse of the same chapter: *"Sin is lawlessness."* In John's usage here, sin is the conscious doing of what is known to be contrary to the will of God. Of course, one who is begotten of God may do that which is contrary to the will of God but which he does not know is contrary to the will of God; therefore, he does not sin in the strict sense in which *"sin"* is used here. Afterward, when he comes to know the will of God, he will see that it is wrong and will confess and forsake it. However, anyone who is begotten of God will not be making a practice of doing what is known to be contrary to the will of God.

Now, it is plain that there is no contradiction between what John actually said in the sixth and ninth verses of 1 John 3 and what John actually said in the eighth and tenth verses of 1 John 1. In the eighth verse, he said, *"If we say that we have no sin, we deceive ourselves."* This does not mean that anyone who says he is not sinning at the present moment, that he is not doing what he knows at the present moment is contrary to the will of God, is deceiving himself. There are certainly moments when we can say that we are not doing what we know is contrary to the will of God. But what John said is that if a man says he has no sins to be forgiven, no sins to be cleansed by the blood of Jesus (see 1 John 1:7–9), that is, that he has never sinned, he deceives himself, and the truth is not in him.

In the tenth verse, John added, *"If we say that we have not sinned,"* we not only deceive ourselves but *"we make* [God] *a liar, and His word is not in us."* A person may not be practicing sin at the present moment—and if a person is born of God, he will not be practicing sin at the present moment—but nevertheless, he has sinned in the past. If he says he has not, he makes God a liar, and God's Word is not in him. The reconciliation here, as in every other apparent contradiction in the Bible, is found by looking at exactly what the inspired authors said.

PRAYER

Q: How do you know God answers prayer?

A: I know it, first of all, because the Bible says so, and I have conclusive proof that the Bible is the inerrant Word of God.* Whatever the Bible says is true, I know is true. The Bible abounds in statements that God answers prayer. For example, Jesus said in Matthew 7:11, *"If you then, being evil, know how to give good gifts to your children, how much more will your Father who is in heaven give good things to those who ask Him!"* He also said to His disciples who were united to Him by a living faith and obedient love, *"Whatever you ask in My name, that I will do, that the Father may be glorified in the Son. If you ask anything in My name, I will do it"* (John 14:13–14).

However, I also know that God answers prayer because He has answered *mine*. Time and time again, throughout the years, I have asked God for things that He alone could give, for things that there was no probability whatsoever of my getting through human effort. I have told no one else of my need, and God has given me the very things for which I asked. There have been times in my life when I have asked God for specific things, and it has been so evident that if I received them, they must be from Him, that I have said to Him in asking for them, "If you will give me this thing, I will never doubt you again as long as I live"—and God has given me the very

---

*See R. A. Torrey, *Powerful Faith* (New Kensington, PA: Whitaker House, 1996).

thing for which I asked. On one occasion, in answer to prayer, God gave six thousand dollars within two hours. On another occasion, when another person and I prayed for five thousand dollars for the Moody Bible Institute in Chicago, word was received by telegram that five thousand dollars had been given to the Institute by a man whom I had never heard of and who lived about one thousand miles from the place where we had prayed. This man had never given a penny to the Moody Bible Institute before and has never given a penny since. I could relate many instances of this kind.

Now, it may be said that this kind of thing is merely a coincidence, but the "coincidence" has occurred so often and there has been such an evident connection between prayer (the cause) and the answer (the effect), that to say it is coincidence is to be unscientific.

The history of George Müller's orphan homes in Bristol, England, is, to a fair-minded investigator of facts, clear proof that God answers prayer. About two thousand children at these orphanages were housed, clothed, and fed over a long period of years in answer to prayer. No money was ever solicited, no debt was ever incurred, and no meal ever failed—even though, up to the very last moment, it often seemed as if it might fail. If anyone studies the facts in connection with George Müller's orphan homes and still doubts that God answers prayer, he is not only willfully obstinate in his unbelief but is also thoroughly unscientific in his treatment of demonstrated facts.

Q: When we pray, is this not asking God to change a law of nature that He established?

A: It is not. Even an earthly father can answer the prayers of his children without changing the laws of nature. Certainly, then, the heavenly Father, who made the laws, can answer prayer. God is not the servant of His own laws; His own laws are His servants. If it were necessary to change them in order to answer prayer, He could do that; however, it is not necessary. For a long time, I lived by prayer; everything I had came in answer to prayer. I know God answered my prayers, but I have no reason to suppose that He changed one single law of nature to do it. The laws of nature do not govern God. They are simply God's fixed way of acting, fixed by His own free choice. (For a related discussion, please refer to the section "Miracles" in this book.)

Q: Why should we tell God our needs when He knows them in advance?

A: We should tell God our needs because He has told us to do so (Philippians 4:6), and because in this way we are taught what we most need to know—our absolute dependence upon God. There are many things that even an earthly father would give his children if they asked for them, that he would not give them if they did not ask for them. It is for the good of the children that they be required to ask. I, for one, am very glad that there are some things that God has withheld from me until I have asked for them.

Q: To whom may I properly address prayer—to God the Father only? Is it right to pray to Jesus Christ and to the Holy Spirit?

A: The normal order of prayer is to the Father, through the Son, in the Spirit (Ephesians 2:18). It is through Christ that we come to God (Hebrews 7:25). God the Father is the ultimate person to whom we pray.

However, there is abundant precedent in the Scriptures for praying to Jesus Christ. In Acts 7:59, when Stephen was filled with the Spirit, we find him calling upon the Lord Jesus. In 2 Corinthians 12:8–9, Paul told us that he implored the Lord three times for a certain thing, and the context shows that the Lord he implored was Christ. In 2 Timothy 2:22, Christians are spoken of as *"those who call on the Lord,"* and verse eight of 2 Timothy 4 shows that the Lord who was meant is the Lord Jesus. In 1 Corinthians 1:2, Christians are described as those who *"call on the name of Jesus Christ our Lord."* We are told in Romans 10:12–13 that *"the same Lord over all is rich to all who call upon Him,"* and in verse nine, we are told that the Lord of whom Paul was speaking is the Lord Jesus.

Regarding praying to the Holy Spirit, there is only one instance recorded in the Bible in which a person directly addressed the Holy Spirit—when God commanded Ezekiel to prophesy to the *"breath"* to breathe on the dry bones so that they would live (Ezekiel 37:9). However, the Scriptures refer to our having communion with the Holy Spirit (2 Corinthians 13:14). Furthermore, Jesus taught that, after His departure, another Comforter would come to take His place, and that this other Comforter is the Holy Spirit (John 14:16–17 KJV; 15:26 KJV). We are dependent upon the Holy Spirit for everything; therefore, we must look to Him—which implies prayer. Yet it is the Father and the Son who give the Holy Spirit (John 15:26; Acts 2:33), and it would seem that if we want the Holy Spirit, instead of praying directly to Him, we should pray to the Father or Son for Him.

Q: Why aren't all our prayers answered?

A: For various reasons. Some of our prayers are not answered because we ourselves are not right with God and in a position where God can wisely answer our prayers. (See 1 Peter 3:7.)

Some of our prayers are not answered because they are not offered in the name of Jesus Christ. In other words, we need to depend on Christ's claims on God and not our own. We have no claims on God. If we approach Him on the basis of our own merit, we will get nothing.

Some of our prayers are not answered because they are not wise and therefore are not in accordance with the will of God (1 John 5:14–15).

Some of our prayers are not answered because we do not persist in prayer. (See Luke 11:5–10; 18:1–8.)

Finally, James 4:2–3 says, *"You do not have because you do not ask. You ask and do not receive, because you ask amiss."*

Q: If the Lord did not answer your prayers, what would you think was the matter? Would you think it was yourself?

A: Most assuredly, I would. I would get alone with God and ask Him to search me by His Spirit and His Word. If He brought anything to light that was displeasing to Him, I would confess it as a sin and forsake it. If He did not bring anything to light, I would continue praying, for I have learned that God does not always give us the best things the first time we ask for them. He tries and develops our faith and teaches us persistence by keeping us waiting. The longer I live, the more I feel that the teaching of Luke 18:1, *"Men always ought to pray and not lose heart,"* is of the highest importance and should sink deeply into our hearts.

There was a time when God did not answer my prayers. I was living solely by faith at the time;

that is, everything I got came in answer to prayer. However, the supplies stopped. I cried to God but got no answer. Then I looked up to God and asked Him to search my heart and bring to light anything in my life that displeased Him. He brought to light something that had often troubled me before but which I would not admit was sin. That night, I said, "O God, if this is wrong, I will give it up," but I got no answer. In the bottom of my heart, I knew it was wrong all the time. Then I said, "O God, this is wrong; it is sin. I will give it up," and the answer came. The fault was in me, not in God. There is nothing that God delights to do more than to answer prayer.

Q: How should I pray in order to get what I ask for?

A: You should follow these guidelines:

♦ First, you must be the kind of person that the Bible describes as the one whose prayers God answers. This is a person who believes in the Lord Jesus Christ with a living faith and shows the reality of his faith by living a life of daily obedience to His will. (See John 14:13–15; 15:7; 1 John 3:22.)

♦ Second, you must pray to the Father, through the Son, in the Spirit (Ephesians 2:18). Much that is called prayer is not really prayer to God. There is no thought of God in the mind, no real approach to God in the heart. It is only on the ground of the shed blood of Jesus Christ that one can really approach God and be sure that his prayers are heard (Hebrews 10:19–20). It is only when we pray in the Holy Spirit, that is, under His guidance, that we pray in such a way that we may be sure that God will hear (Jude 20; Romans 8:26–27).

♦ Third, you must pray according to the will of God (1 John 5:14–15). We may know the will of God by studying the Word, which is given to us to reveal God's will, and by the leading of the Spirit. Whenever you ask for anything that is promised in the Word of God, you may know that it is the will of God to give it, and He will give what you ask.

♦ Fourth, you must pray persistently (Luke 11:5–10; 18:1–8). Here is where many fail. They do not "pray through." They pray for a thing once or twice and then conclude it is not God's will to give it. God demands of us a persistent faith that will not take no for an answer. Many people pray and pray up to the very point of getting something, and then they fail because they do not pray through.

PREDESTINATION

Q: How do you reconcile man's freedom of choice with God's foreknowledge and foreordination? Also, please explain the meaning of this verse: "[Jesus], *being delivered by the determined purpose and foreknowledge of God, you have taken by lawless hands, have crucified, and put to death"* (Acts 2:23).

A: The above verse means that the actions of Judas and the rest who betrayed Jesus and put Him to death were taken into God's plan and were thus made a part of it. But it does not mean that these men were not perfectly free in their choice. They did not do as they did because God knew that they would do so, but the fact that they would do so was the basis upon which God knew it. Foreknowledge no more determines a man's actions than after-knowledge. Knowledge is determined by fact, not fact by knowledge.

Practically the same explanation applies to Romans 8:29: *"Whom He foreknew, He also predestined to be conformed to the image of His Son."*

Q: Please explain Acts 13:48: *"And as many as had been appointed to eternal life believed."* Are some born to be lost?

A: God knows from all eternity what each person will do—whether he will yield to the Spirit and accept Christ or whether he will resist the Spirit and refuse Christ. Those who will receive Him are ordained to eternal life. If any are lost, it is simply because they will not come to Christ and thus obtain life (John 5:40). *"Whoever desires"* may come (Revelation 22:17), and all who do come will be received (John 6:37).

God does not ordain anyone to be lost against his own will. But in God's infinite wisdom and holiness, it is ordained that whoever deliberately and persistently rejects His glorious Son will be banished forever from His presence.

PROSPERITY OF THE WICKED

Q: How is it that a holy and just God allows the wicked to prosper while the good often suffer poverty?

A: What we call prosperity is often in reality a curse. On the other hand, poverty is often a great blessing. God allows the good to suffer poverty because that is what they need most, all things taken into consideration. One of the things that I often thank God for is that the large amount of money that I expected to inherit from my father never came to me and that, at one time, I was allowed to suffer extreme poverty. I have known what it means to be in a foreign country with a wife and child, in a strange city where the people spoke a strange language, and with my money all gone. I now thank God for it. It may have seemed hard at the time, but it brought great blessing. Poverty drives men nearer to God, makes them feel more deeply their dependence upon Him. It is not something to be dreaded but something to thank God for.

The psalmist was confronted with this same perplexity. He said in Psalm 73:3, *"I was envious of the boastful, when I saw the prosperity of the wicked."* In the twelfth and thirteenth verses, he added, *"Behold, these are the ungodly, who are always at ease; they increase in riches. Surely I have cleansed my heart in vain, and washed my hands in innocence."* But later on in the psalm, he told us that all his perplexity was solved when he went into the sanctuary of God—when he communed with God. The mystery was then explained to him. He understood the end of the wicked; he saw how their prosperity is just for a moment, how God has set them in slippery places, and how they are brought to desolation in a moment. On the other hand, he discovered of himself, and of the righteous in general, that even in their poverty they are continually with God. God upholds them. Down in this world of testing and trial, He guides us with His counsel, and when we come out of the fire purified, He afterward receives us into His glory (vv. 16–24).

Much of our difficulty comes from the fact that we forget that this world is not everything, that this brief world is simply a preparation for a future eternal world. We forget that happy is the man who has his bad things in this life but in the eternal life to come has his good things, and wretched indeed is the man who has his good things in this life and his bad things in that eternal world that is to come (Luke 16:25).

PURGATORY

Q: Is the doctrine of purgatory scriptural?

A: The Scriptures do teach that there is an intermediate state after death, but this is not purgatory. Please refer to the following sections in this book: "Afterlife" and "Salvation, after Death."

RELIGION

Q: What difference does it make what religion a person professes, provided he does the best he can?

A: It makes all the difference in the world. Christianity is true. Other religious are false, though they may have elements of truth in them. It does not make a lie any less a lie to believe it most sincerely. Indeed, the more sincerely and heartily a person believes a lie, the worse off he is. I may believe that poison is food, and believe it very sincerely, but if I take it, it will kill me just as quickly as it would if I had known it was poison. Consider another example. If I get on the wrong train, a train that is going in the opposite direction from my destination, it will not take me to my desired destination no matter how sincerely and earnestly I believe it is going there. It is the truth that sets men free when they believe it (John 8:32), and no amount of earnest faith in an error will set a person free. Indeed, the more earnestly a person believes error, the more it will enslave him.

There is no more foolish idea in the world today than that it does not make any difference what a person believes, as long as he is sincere. What a person really believes determines what he is. If he believes error, he will be wrong, not only for the life that is to come but also for this present life, no matter how seriously or earnestly he believes it.

THE RESURRECTION OF THE BODY

Q: How is it possible that we will rise again with the same bodies we had on earth?

A: It is not possible. The Bible distinctly teaches that there will be a resurrection of the body. However, it does not teach that we will rise again with the same body we had on earth. It clearly teaches that we will not rise with the same body. In 1 Corinthians 15:37–38, we are told, *"And what you sow, you do not sow that body that shall be, but mere grain; perhaps wheat or some other* *grain. But God gives it a body as He pleases, and to each seed its own body."* In verse 42, we read, *"So also is the resurrection of the dead."* In other words—as the context clearly shows—just as grain that is sown rises up as a different kind of body, so it will be in the resurrection of the dead. The body that rises will not be the very body that was buried, though it will be the outcome of that body. It will not be composed of exactly the same material elements that were laid in the grave; nevertheless, it will be a body, a real body. As it says in 1 Corinthians 15:42–44, the bodies we now have will be *"sown in corruption"* but will be *"raised in incorruption."* They will be *"sown in dishonor"* but will be *"raised in glory."* They will be *"sown in weakness"* but will be *"raised in power."* They will be *"sown a natural body"* but will be *"raised a spiritual body. There is a natural body, and there is a spiritual body."*

Q: What kind of a body will we have in the resurrection?

A: It will not be flesh and blood (1 Corinthians 15:50–53); on the other hand, it will not be pure spirit but will have flesh and bones (Luke 24:39). It will be incorruptible—not subject to decay, imperishable, glorious, powerful (1 Corinthians 15:42–43). The days of weariness and weakness will be gone forever. The body will be able to accomplish everything the spirit purposes. It will be luminous, shining, dazzling, bright like the sun (Matthew 13:43; Daniel 12:3; compare Matthew 17:2; Luke 9:29). Resurrection bodies will differ from one another. (See 1 Corinthians 15:41–42.) The resurrection body will be the consummation of our adoption, our placing as sons (Romans 8:23). In the resurrection body, it will be outwardly manifest that we are sons of God. Before His incarnation, Christ was *"in the form of God"* (Philippians 2:6), that is, in the visible appearance of God. The word translated *"form"* means the external appearance—that with which something strikes the outward vision. In the resurrection, we also will be in the visible appearance of God. (See Colossians 3:4 RV; 1 John 3:2 RV.)

REWARDS

Q: Is it scriptural for a Christian to work for reward?

A: It certainly is. The Bible constantly holds out rewards, both temporal and eternal, for faithful service. Our Lord Jesus Himself told us to store up treasures in heaven (Matthew 6:19–21). The Christian should serve not merely for the reward but also out of love for Jesus Christ. However, he has a right to expect a reward, and the reward is a great incentive to faithful service.

THE SABBATH

Q: Why was the Jewish Sabbath, or the seventh day of the week that God commanded to be observed as the Sabbath day (Exodus 20:8–11), changed to the first day of the week—what we call the Lord's Day? Why is this day now observed as the Christian Sabbath?

A: Let me say, first of all, that there is no commandment in the Ten Commandments that says the Israelites were to keep the seventh day of the week. The words *of the week* were added by man to the commandment as given by God. What God really commanded through Moses was: *"Six days you shall labor and do all your work, but the seventh day is the Sabbath of the LORD your God"* (Exodus 20:9–10). It does not say that the Sabbath is the seventh day of the week; it says that the Sabbath is the seventh day after six days of labor. Whether we keep the seventh day of the week or the first day of the week, we are keeping the fourth commandment to the very letter. If one is a Jew belonging to the "old creation," let him keep the seventh day of the week. But if he is a Christian and standing on resurrection ground, let him keep the first day of the week, Resurrection Day.

Second, the Jewish Sabbath was not changed to the Lord's Day. While both the Jewish Sabbath and the Lord's Day are a literal keeping of the fourth commandment, they are not the same day, and they do not stand for the same idea. One belongs to the old creation, the other to the new. (See 2 Corinthians 5:17; Galatians 6:15; Hebrews 9:11.) It has sometimes been said by certain Christians that there is no authority for the change and that the Roman Catholic Church or the pope made the change. This statement is absolutely untrue. History proves that Christians kept the first day of the week long before there was any Roman Catholic Church. We have indications that they kept it in New Testament times. It was on the first day of the week that the early disciples came together to break bread (Acts 20:7). It was on the first day of the week that believers put aside money for the needs of other Christians (1 Corinthians 16:2). In the writings of the early church Fathers, long before the Roman Catholic Church had developed and, of course, long before there was any pope, we find it stated again and again that the first day of the week was the one that Christians observed.

The apostle Paul explicitly taught that a Christian should not allow himself to be judged in regard to the Jewish Sabbath, and that the Jewish Sabbath belongs with other Jewish observances concerning meat and drink, holy days, new moons, and so forth (Colossians 2:16). These were the *"shadow of things to come,"* but the substance is in Christ (v. 17).

SALVATION AFTER DEATH

Q: Luke 15:4 says, *"What man of you, having a hundred sheep, if he loses one of them, does not leave the ninety-nine in the wilderness, and go after the one which is lost until he finds it?"* Does this verse give clear proof that Christ is going to continue to seek and to save, after death, the lost who have had a good opportunity on earth to repent and come to Christ?

A: It certainly does not. All that is taught here is that the shepherd goes after the lost sheep until he finds it; but not all men are "sheep." The whole argument that seeks to prove that this verse teaches that all men will ultimately be found and saved proceeds upon the supposition that all men are sheep. But we are distinctly taught in the Word of God that this is not the case. There are sheep and there are goats. (See Matthew 25:31–46.) There are sheep and there are swine and dogs. (See 2 Peter 2:20–22.)

Undoubtedly, Jesus Christ will find every one of His sheep sooner or later. The Bible teaches that He will find them in this present life. But the Bible also teaches that some men are goats and will remain goats up to the Judgment Day. Christ will say to the goats, *"Depart from Me, you cursed, into the everlasting fire prepared for the devil and his angels"* (Matthew 25:41). These are the words of Jesus Himself.

Q: First Peter 3:18–20 reads: *"For Christ also suffered once for sins, the just for the unjust, that He might bring us to God, being put to death in the flesh but made alive by the Spirit, by whom also He went and preached to the spirits in prison, who formerly were disobedient, when once the Divine longsuffering waited in the days of Noah, while the ark was being prepared."* Does this not teach that there is another opportunity to repent after death?

A: It certainly does not. It does teach that Christ, when He was put to death in the flesh (that is, in His body), was quickened in His spirit, and in His spirit went and preached to the *"spirits in prison."* But we are not told that the spirits in prison were men who had lived on the earth and died in their sin. There is reason to suppose that they were the angels who were disobedient in the time of Noah. (See verse 20; 2 Peter 2:4; Genesis 6:1–2; Jude 6–7.) But even supposing that they were the departed spirits of men who had died in sin, we are not told that Jesus preached the Gospel to them. The word translated *"preached"* in this passage does not mean "to preach the Gospel," but "to herald." There is another word often used in the New Testament that means "to preach the Gospel," and it is significant that this word is not used in this passage. Nor are we told that any of these *"spirits in prison"* to whom Christ preached repented, or even could repent. The passage simply teaches that the kingdom has been proclaimed in hell as well as in heaven.

Q: Is there any word of Scripture that gives us grounds to believe in repentance after death?

A: There is not.

SANCTIFICATION

Q: Some teach that a believer is sanctified instantaneously. Others declare that sanctification is a gradual process, perfected in heaven only. What does the Bible teach regarding this?

A: The Bible teaches that every believer is sanctified instantly, the moment he believes in Jesus Christ (1 Corinthians 1:2; 6:11). The moment anyone becomes a member of the church of God by faith in Christ Jesus—in that moment—he is sanctified. *"Through the offering of the body of Jesus Christ once for all"* (Hebrews 10:10), we are cleansed forever from all the guilt of sin. We are *"perfected forever"* (v. 14), as far as our standing before God is concerned. The sacrifice does not need to be repeated, as the Jewish sacrifices were. The work is done *"once for all."* Sin is put away forever (Hebrews 9:25–28; see Galatians 3:13), and we are sanctified—"set apart"— forever as God's special and eternal possession.

In this sense, every believer is instantly sanctified the moment he believes in Jesus.

However, there is still another sense in which every believer may be instantly sanctified. It is his privilege and his duty to present his whole body as a *"living sacrifice"* (Romans 12:1) to God. Such an offering is well pleasing to God; when it is made, God sends down the fire of the Holy Spirit and takes to Himself what is thus presented. Then, instantly, the believer, so far as his will is concerned, is wholly God's, or perfectly sanctified.

But after he is perfectly sanctified in this sense, he may discover, and undoubtedly often will, as he studies the Word of God and as he is taught by the Holy Spirit, that there are individual acts and habits of his life, forms of feeling, speech, and action, that are not in conformity with this central purpose of his life. These should be confessed to God as sinful and should be renounced. In this way, these areas of his life will also be brought by the Holy Spirit into conformity with the will of God as revealed in His Word. But the victory in these newly discovered and unclaimed territories may also be instantaneous. There is no need for a prolonged battle. For example, if I were to discover in myself an irritability that was clearly displeasing to God, I could go to God at once and confess it and renounce it. In an instant, not by my own strength but by looking to Jesus and by surrendering this department of my life to the control of the Holy Spirit, I could overcome it and never have another failure in that way.

Yet, while there is this instantaneous sanctification that any child of God may claim at any moment, there is also a progressive work of sanctification—an increasing in love (1 Thessalonians 3:12; 4:9–10); an abounding more and more in a godly walk and in pleasing God (1 Thessalonians 4:1); a growing in the *"grace and knowledge of our Lord and Savior Jesus Christ"* (2 Peter 3:18); a being transformed into the image of our Lord Jesus Christ from glory to glory, each new gaze at Him making us more like Him (2 Corinthians 3:18); and a growing up into Christ in all things until we mature into a full-grown man, *"to the measure of the stature of the fullness of Christ"* (Ephesians 4:13; see also verses 11–15).

Sanctification becomes complete in the fullest sense at the coming of our Lord and Savior Jesus Christ (1 Thessalonians 3:13; 5:23). It is not in this present life or at death, but at the coming of Christ, that we are entirely sanctified in this fullest sense.

THE SECOND COMING OF JESUS CHRIST

Q: Does the Bible teach that Jesus Christ is coming back to this earth personally and visibly?

A: It does. There is nothing more clearly taught in the Bible than that Jesus Christ is coming back to this earth personally, bodily, and visibly. In Acts 1:10–11, we read that two men in white apparel stood by the disciples as they gazed steadfastly into heaven at Jesus as He was being taken up before their eyes. These men in white apparel said to the disciples, *"This same Jesus, who was taken up from you into heaven, will so come in like manner as you saw Him go into heaven"* (v. 11). Now, they had seen Him going into heaven personally, bodily, visibly, and they were told that He would come back just as He had gone.

An attempt has been made by those who deny the personal return of our Lord to say that *"in like manner"* means "with equal certainty," but the Greek words translated *"so...in like manner"* permit no such construction. They are never used in that way. Literally translated, they mean, "thus in the manner which," and are never used to describe anything but the manner, the precise manner, in which a thing is done. Jesus Christ is coming back exactly as the disciples saw Him going: personally, bodily, visibly.

The same truth is taught in John 14:3, 1 Thessalonians 4:16–17, and many other passages. In Hebrews 9:28, we are told, *"So Christ was offered once to bear the sins of many. To those who eagerly wait for Him He will appear a second time, apart from sin, for salvation."* Translated literally, the word in this passage that is translated *"will appear"* would be "will be seen." It is a word used only of seeing with the eye. In Revelation 1:7, we read, *"Behold, He is coming with clouds, and every eye will see Him, even they who pierced Him. And all the tribes of the earth will mourn because of Him."*

These very plain promises cannot, by any fair system of interpretation, be made to refer to the coming of Christ in the Holy Spirit, as some would say. The coming of the Holy Spirit is, in a very real sense, the coming of Christ. (See John 14:15–18, 21–23.) However, it is not the Coming referred to in the above passages, and cannot be made such except by perverting the plain words of God. Nor is the Coming described in these passages the coming of Christ to receive the believer at the time of his death. The details given do not fit the death of the believer. Nor do these passages refer to the coming of Christ at the destruction of Jerusalem in A.D. 70. The destruction of Jerusalem was, in a sense, a precursor, prophecy, and type of the Judgment at the end of the age; therefore, in Matthew 24:3–31 and Mark 13:3–27, these two events are described in connection with one another. But God's judgment on Jerusalem was clearly not the event referred to in Acts 1 and the other passages given above. The second coming of Jesus Christ, which is so frequently mentioned in the New Testament, is the great hope of the church, and it is still mentioned as lying in the future. (See 1 Corinthians 11:26; John 21:22–23; Revelation 1:7; 22:20.)

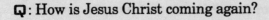

Q: How is Jesus Christ coming again?

A: As I already mentioned, He is coming personally, visibly, and bodily. But in addition to this, He is coming very publicly (Matthew 24:26–27; Revelation 1:7). Every now and then, someone appears in some corner of the earth who is announced to be Christ in His second coming, but these obscure, "inner room" christs (see Matthew 24:26) are all frauds that have long since been predicted and discredited. Christ is *"coming on the clouds of heaven with power and great glory"* (v. 30). He is coming in the glory of His Father with the holy angels. (See Matthew 16:27; Mark 8:38; 2 Thessalonians 1:7.) He is coming unannounced, without warning, unexpectedly, suddenly. (See Matthew 24:37–39; Luke 21:34–35; 1 Thessalonians 5:2–3; Revelation 16:15.)

Q: Do you believe that the second coming of Christ is near at hand? If so, why? What should we do to prepare for Him?

A: As far as I know, our Lord may return again any day. There is no event predicted in Scripture that must occur before Jesus comes to receive His own to Himself, although it seems as if there are some events that must occur before He comes to the earth with His saints. (See 2 Thessalonians 2:1–4, 8.) As far as we know, He may come for us believers at any moment, and He Himself has commanded us always to be ready because *"the*

Son of Man is coming at an hour you do not expect" (Matthew 24:44).

Furthermore, there seem to be indications that *"the coming of the Lord is at hand"* (James 5:8). Second Timothy 3:1–5 gives a very accurate description of our own time. The increase of unbelief in the professing church and in the pulpit, the growing unrest in the social and political world, the apparently rapid development of the Antichrist—all these things seem to point to the near approach of our Lord. But we should bear in mind that earnest men of God and students of the Bible have often thought in times past that the coming of the Lord was very near. In a sense it was, and they were not mistaken. Those who thought it was so far away that they allowed it to have no effect on their lives were the ones who were really mistaken.

Today, men's hearts are *"failing them from fear and the expectation of those things which are coming on the earth"* (Luke 21:26). But when the true believer and intelligent student of the Word sees these things begin to come to pass, he will not be discouraged. He will lift up his head and look up because he will know that his redemption is drawing near (v. 28). We should all be dressed and ready and have our lamps burning (Luke 12:35), and we should be like men who wait for their master to return from a wedding so that when He does come and knock, we may open to Him immediately (v. 36).

Q: What is the logical and adequate explanation of Matthew 16:28, where Jesus said, *"Assuredly, I say to you, there are some standing here who shall not taste death till they see the Son of Man coming in His kingdom"*?

A: The answer to this question is evident if one continues reading, ignoring the chapter division between the sixteenth and seventeenth chapters of Matthew. This division is not part of the original Scriptures but is an editor's addition, and sometimes these divisions are made in illogical ways. It is noticeably so in this case.

After quoting the words in question, Matthew goes on to describe the Transfiguration of Christ. In this Transfiguration, Jesus, the Son of Man, was seen *"coming in His kingdom."* He was manifested in the glory that is properly His. If things had taken their natural course, He would have been glorified then and there, without going through death. However, He turned His back on that glory and went down from the mountain to meet the awful tragedy of His death, the only way in which He could redeem men. It was of *"His decease* [that is, His atoning death]*"* (Luke 9:31) that Moses and Elijah spoke with Him when they appeared with Him in the glory. This Transfiguration, seen by some who were standing with Him when He spoke the words found in Matthew 16:28, was the Son of Man seen coming in His kingdom.

SECRET SOCIETIES

Q: Do you believe in secret societies? Do you think it is wise to publicly expose them through preaching?

A: I do not believe in secret societies, and I believe it is wise to show young Christians the danger of them. This ought to be done wisely. I do not believe in making a hobby of this sort of thing. I would not start by attacking lodges; the first thing I would do would be to get men and women converted to Jesus Christ.

Q: Should a Christian retain membership in a secret society?

A: No. I do not see how a Christian who intelligently studies his Bible can do so. The Bible tells us plainly, *"Do not be unequally yoked together with unbelievers. For what fellowship has righteousness with lawlessness? And what communion has light with darkness?"* (2 Corinthians 6:14). All secret societies of which I have any knowledge are made up, at least partly, of unbelievers—that is, of those who have not accepted Jesus Christ and surrendered their wills to God. In light of this express commandment in God's Word, I do not see how a Christian can retain membership in them. I am not saying that no members of secret societies are

Christians, for I have known a great many excellent Christians who were members of secret societies. However, I cannot see how they can continue to be so. Many continue as members of the Masonic and similar orders simply because they are not acquainted with the teachings of the Word of God on the subject.

Furthermore, in the rituals of some secret societies, the Scriptures themselves are perverted. The name of Jesus Christ is cut out of passages in which it occurs in the Bible so as not to offend Jews and other non-Christians. How a Christian can retain membership in a society that thus deceitfully handles the Word of God, and, above all, cuts out the name of his Lord and Master, I cannot understand.

Still further, oaths of the most shocking nature are required in some secret societies, and there are ceremonies that are simply a caricature of biblical truths. For example, there is even a mock resurrection scene.

Moreover, Christianity seeks the light and not the darkness (Ephesians 5:8, 11–12). Undoubtedly, many Christians go into the Masonic and other orders for the purpose of getting hold of the non-Christian members and winning them for Christ, but this is a mistaken policy. Experience proves that the secret society is more likely to swamp the spiritual life of the Christian than the Christian is to win his fellow Masons to Christ.

SOULWINNING

Q: How may I gain a love for people and a concern for their salvation?

A: In the following way:

♦ First, by giving your whole self up—all your thoughts, feelings, ambitions, purposes—to the control of the Holy Spirit. The Holy Spirit loves people, and if you will give yourself up to His control, He will impart to you a love for people. The very first part of the description of the fruit of the Spirit is love (Galatians 5:22).

♦ Second, by dwelling on the actual condition of men who are outside of Christ, as revealed in the Word of God, and by studying what the Word of God says about their ultimate destiny. If you will reflect upon the hell that awaits lost souls, you will soon (if you are a Christian at all) have a passion for their salvation.

♦ Third, by observing Jesus Christ and dwelling on His conduct toward the lost.

SPIRITUALISM

Q: Can a Christian be a Spiritualist?

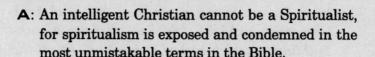

A: An intelligent Christian cannot be a Spiritualist, for spiritualism is exposed and condemned in the most unmistakable terms in the Bible.

Spiritualism is not something modern. It is as old as the days of Moses. The mediums in those days had, or professed to have, familiar spirits who spoke through them. Consulting those who had familiar spirits was condemned by God through Moses in the strongest terms. For example, He said in Leviticus 19:31, *"Give no regard to mediums and familiar spirits; do not seek after them, to be defiled by them: I am the LORD your God."* In Leviticus 20:6, He said, *"And the person who turns to mediums and familiar spirits, to prostitute himself with them, I will set My face against that person and cut him off from his people."* Also, in Deuteronomy 18:10–12, He said, *"There shall not be found among you anyone who makes his son or his daughter pass through the fire, or one who practices witchcraft, or a soothsayer, or one who interprets omens, or a sorcerer, or one who conjures spells, or a medium, or a spiritist, or one who calls up the dead. For all who do these things are an abomination to the LORD, and because of these abominations the LORD your God drives them* [the Canaanites] *out from before you."*

One of the strongest charges brought against Manasseh, king of Judah, was that he was a Spiritualist, and thus provoked God to anger (2 Kings 21:1–2, 6). Saul lost his kingdom and his head for consulting a medium. We read in 1 Chronicles 10:13–14: *"So Saul died for his unfaithfulness which he had committed against the LORD, because he did not keep the word of the LORD, and also because he consulted a medium for guidance. But he did not inquire of the LORD; therefore He killed him, and turned the kingdom over to David the son of Jesse."*

Nearly all so-called modern spiritualism is a fraud. The tricks of the mediums have been exposed time and time again. Still, probably not all of it is fraud. While there is a natural explanation for most of the manifestations of modern spiritualism, and while most of these manifestations are done through deception, some of them do seem to have a supernatural origin. We must remember, however, that just because something is supernatural, this does not necessarily prove that it is right or true. According to the teaching of the Bible, there is a real, unseen world, a world of spirits, but some of the spirits are bad; they are emissaries and agents of the Devil (Ephesians 6:12; 2 Thessalonians 2:9–12). The fact that a person can do things and make revelations that we cannot explain by natural causes— things and revelations that seem to show he is particularly in contact with the supernatural world—does not prove that he is in league with God. Rather, it may prove that he is in league with the Devil. It may be that spirits do manifest themselves, but it does not follow that they are the spirits of our departed friends or other good and wise people who have left this world. There is good reason to believe that these spirits who come to us pretending to be the spirits of our loved ones who have departed are demonic spirits.

A prominent medium, who was at the time operating in Chicago, once came to me and said, "Mr. Torrey, these things are not all sleight of hand and trickery. There are spirits, but they are demons. I was tormented all last night by the demons through whom I do my work." I asked him why he did not renounce the whole business. He replied that he was making a splendid living through it and knew of no other way in which he could do so well. A friend of mine who dabbled in spiritualism and developed unusual powers as a medium was afterward led to renounce the whole business. He went into it thinking it was all right, but he had not gone far before he found it was demonic. There have been many instances of the same thing.

Even if the spirits manifested are the spirits of our departed loved ones, we are commanded in the Bible not to seek knowledge in this way (Isaiah 8:19–20). Whoever dabbles in spiritualism at all enters the Devil's territory and disobeys the most explicit commandments of God.

The spiritual and moral influence of spiritualism is ruinous. Sooner or later, it leads to the renouncing of Jesus Christ and to all kinds of immorality. When we lose our loved ones, the temptation often becomes strong to seek communication with them, and well-meaning people are led into spiritualism in this way. But it is a snare of the Devil and leads to the eternal ruin of the soul.

TROUBLE

Q: Does trouble come from God? Do you believe that God ever sends trouble to us purposely, or that it comes in the natural order of events?

A: What we call "the natural order of events" is God's ordering. God controls all things. Every detail of our history is in His hands, and what appears to us most natural and inevitable is just as much a part of His will as what we believe is a direct intervention on His part.

God undoubtedly permits trouble to come to us sometimes. He permits it to come when He sees that we need it. He would prevent its coming if He saw that we did not need it. If we would surrender our wills to God, we would not need trouble as a discipline or chastening, which we do need when our wills are not surrendered, and we would therefore escape a great amount of misfortune. If we would more quickly learn God's purposes in the troubles that come to us, we would more quickly be relieved of them. For example, undoubtedly, many people are sick who might be well if they would only learn the lesson that God is trying to teach them by the sickness and then look to Him for recovery. I have known people who were in trouble for months or years, and who suddenly were delivered from it when they learned to surrender their wills absolutely to God and to rejoice in His will—whatever it might be—and then looked to Him so that they might be delivered for His glory.

Satan, as a source of our troubles, is also under God's control. See, for example, the cases of Job (Job 1:12; 2:6) and Paul (2 Corinthians 12:7–9).

THE UNPARDONABLE SIN

Q: What is the "unpardonable sin"? Can a person be saved who has committed it? What is the sin against the Holy Spirit?

A: The sin against the Holy Spirit, or, as it is usually called, the "unpardonable sin," is mentioned in Matthew 12:31–32. If you will look at these verses carefully, in context, you will see that it means blasphemy against the Spirit. That is, it is the deliberate attributing to the Devil what is known to be the work of the Holy Spirit. The Pharisees knew in their innermost hearts that what Jesus was doing, He was doing by the power of the Spirit of God (see verse 28), but they were not willing to accept Jesus and His claims. In their opposition to Him, they deliberately attributed to the Devil, *"Beelzebub"* (v. 24), what in their innermost hearts they knew to be the work of the Spirit of God.

If one commits this sin, he passes beyond the possibility of repentance. He becomes so hardened in sin that he will not come to Jesus. His eternal destiny is sealed.

The great majority of people who imagine they have committed this unpardonable sin really have not. If anyone has a desire to repent and turn to Christ, that in itself is proof that he has not committed it. We have Jesus' own word for it that whoever comes to Him, He will *"by no means cast out"* (John 6:37).

Q: Some years ago, I was converted and led a happy Christian life for some time. Then I fell into sin. Now I am in despair, for I think that my case is the one described in Hebrews 6:4–6, and that it is impossible to renew me again to repentance. Is there any hope for me?

A: Yes, there is every hope for you if you will come to Jesus. He said in John 6:37, *"The one who comes to Me I will by no means cast out."* He did not say, "He who was never converted and who comes to Me, I will by no means cast out." He said, *"The one **who comes to Me** I will by no means cast out."* It is evident that you have a desire to come. It is as plain as day in God's Word that God desires you to come. (See Matthew 11:29–30; Revelation 22:17.) Therefore, just come, and you have Jesus' own word for it that He will receive you!

Hebrews 6:4–6 does not describe your situation at all. See how it reads: *"For it is impossible for those who were once enlightened, and have tasted the heavenly gift, and have become partakers of the Holy Spirit, and have tasted the good word of God and the powers of the age to come, if they fall away, to renew them again to repentance, since they crucify again for themselves the Son of God, and put Him to an open shame."*

The difficulty with the one described here is that it is impossible to renew him again to repentance, and that is the reason why he cannot be saved. But you show that you desire to repent. The words in Hebrews 6:4–6 were written to Jewish Christians who were suffering persecution and who were therefore in danger of apostatizing and renouncing Christ and going back to Judaism. The Holy Spirit was warning them that if they did, after all the light they had had, there would no longer be hope for them because it would be impossible to renew them again to repentance. Later on in the chapter, the writer said that he did not expect any of them to do what is described (Hebrews 6:9). The warning itself would help to keep them from doing it.

This passage in Hebrews 6, therefore, does not describe merely a backslider. It describes an apostate, one who not only falls into sin but who, after having been enlightened and having tasted the heavenly gift and having been made an actual partaker of the Holy Spirit, falls away, that is, apostatizes. The Greek word translated *"fall away"* in this passage is used in the Greek translation of the Old Testament (the Septuagint) to describe one who has apostatized from God and gone astray after idols. (See Ezekiel 14:13; 15:8.)

That a mere backslider may come back to God is abundantly proven from many Scriptures. (See Jeremiah 3:12–14; Hosea 14:1–4; Luke 15:11–24.) The apostle Peter himself, after having started to follow Christ, sinned most grievously, denying his Lord with oaths and curses, but his Lord received him back and gave him a greater fullness of blessing than he had ever known before. Anyone who has the desire to repent of sin and return to the Lord Jesus may know clearly from this fact that he is not the person described in Hebrews 6:4–6. I have met many people who were in hopeless despair because they thought their situation was described here. However, after being shown the truth of the Lord Jesus' willingness to receive them if they would come back to Him, they have come back and are now happy and useful Christians.

Q: What is meant by Hebrews 10:26: *"If we sin willfully after we have received the knowledge of the truth, there no longer remains a sacrifice for sins"*? Does it mean that if anyone sins knowingly after he has received the knowledge of the truth, there is no longer any hope of pardon or salvation for him?

A: No, it means nothing of the kind. The words translated *"sin willfully"* mean to sin willingly, voluntarily, of one's own accord. Such sin is in contrast to the sins committed inconsiderately or from ignorance or weakness. One may sin *knowingly* without sinning *willfully*. He may know that what he is doing is wrong, and yet he does not do it voluntarily—he does not do it willingly, of his own accord—but because the temptation is too strong for him. The word translated *"willfully"* is the same word used in 1 Peter 5:2, where the contrast is drawn between the one who does his work by constraint and the one who does it out of his own glad choice. There are many who sin knowingly but who do not sin willfully in this sense.

If a person, after receiving the knowledge of the truth, deliberately and of his own choice chooses to sin rather than to obey God, there no longer remains a sacrifice for sins for him—only *"a certain fearful expectation of judgment, and fiery indignation"* (Hebrews 10:27). Such a person will have no desire to repent.

If one has a desire to repent, this fact, in itself, proves that he has not sinned in this way. No one described in Hebrews 10:26 will be seeking light and desiring to come back to God. The very fact that a person asks such a question as this shows that he is not the person described in Hebrews 10:26.

VICTORY OVER SIN

Q: I was converted several years ago, but I am constantly giving way to temptation. I know that my sins are forgiven, but is there any way in which I can have daily victory over sin?

A: There is. The salvation that is offered to us in Jesus Christ is a threefold salvation:

◆ First, there is salvation from the guilt of sin. This we get through the atoning death of Christ on the cross. When Jesus Christ died on the cross of Calvary, He made a perfect atonement for our sins and put them away forever. (See Galatians 3:13; 2 Corinthians 5:21; Hebrews 10:12–14.) The very moment that we accept Him, we are saved from the guilt of sin. Every sin is blotted out. It is just as if we had never sinned. Our standing before God is perfect. We are justified in His sight. (See Acts 10:43; 13:38–39; 2 Corinthians 5:21.)

◆ Second, there is salvation from the power of sin. This we receive through the resurrection of Jesus Christ, who, having risen from the dead and ascended to the right hand of the Father, *"always lives to make intercession for* [us]*"* (Hebrews 7:25). He is *"able to save"* not merely from the uttermost but *"to the uttermost those who come to God through Him"* (v. 25). By His resurrection power in our lives, He gives us victory over the power of temptation and sin day by day. Having been reconciled to God by His death, we are now saved day by day from the power of sin by His life, that is, by His resurrection life (Romans 5:10).

Furthermore, the risen Christ imparts to us His Holy Spirit. What we cannot do in our own strength (namely, overcome sin) the Spirit of God whom the risen Christ gives to dwell in us accomplishes for us (Romans 8:1–4). So then, the way to get daily victory over sin is to stop trying to fight sin in your own strength. Look up to the risen Christ, believing that He has all power in heaven and on earth and that He therefore has power to set you free from the power of sin. Just trust Him to do it.

Additionally, surrender your whole life to the control of the Holy Spirit. Ask Him to come in and take possession of all your desires, all your purposes, all your plans, all your thoughts. He will do it. He will bear His own fruit in your life—*"love, joy, peace, longsuffering, kindness, goodness, faithfulness, gentleness, self-control"* (Galatians 5:22–23). If we *"walk in the Spirit"* (v. 16), that is, submit our whole lives to His control, we will not *"fulfill the lust of the flesh"* (v. 16).

♦ Third, there is salvation from the very presence of sin. This we will obtain through Christ's coming again. This we will enjoy when He does come again, and when we are made perfectly like Him because we see Him as He is (1 John 3:2).

"WHAT WOULD JESUS DO?"

Q: Should the thought, "What would Jesus do?" be the standard for Christian conduct and practice today?

A: It certainly should, and it is the only standard. We read in 1 John 2:6, *"He who says he abides in Him ought himself also to walk just as He walked."* The standard of Christian living is not the Ten Commandments. It is not even the Golden Rule. It is Jesus Himself. Our Lord Jesus gave to His disciples a new law that includes the old but goes far beyond it. The new law is this: *"That you love one another; as I have loved you, that you also love one another"* (John 13:34). If we study the life of Jesus and see what He did under the circumstances in which He lived when He was here on earth, then, under the Spirit's teaching, we can decide what He would do if He were in our circumstances today. The question for the Christian is never "What do other Christians do?" or "What do other Christians tell me to do?" but "What would Jesus want me to do, and what would Jesus Himself do?"

THE WORLD'S CONDITION

Q: Is the world becoming better or worse?

A: If you use the word *world* in the biblical sense, that is, denoting the great body of mankind who reject Jesus Christ, then undoubtedly it is growing worse. The Bible says that *"the whole world* [that is, the whole mass of men excluding those who accept Jesus Christ, who are not of the world (see John 15:19)] *lies under the sway of the wicked one"* (1 John 5:19). Therefore, the world cannot do anything but grow worse all the time it goes on rejecting Christ.

But if, by "the world," you mean the whole human race, there are two developments going on in it—a good development in those who have come out of the world and have accepted Jesus Christ (who are constantly growing better), and an evil development in those who reject Christ (who are constantly growing worse). In outward things, of course, the world is affected more or less by the believers who are in it, and this leads to many reforms. However, the Bible says that *"evil men and impostors will proceed from bad to worse, deceiving and being deceived"* (2 Timothy 3:13 NAS), and that *"in latter times some will depart from the faith, giving heed to deceiving spirits and doctrines of demons"* (1 Timothy 4:1). Second Timothy 3:1–5 says, *"But know this, that in the last days perilous times will come: for men will be lovers of themselves, lovers of money, boasters, proud, blasphemers, disobedient to parents, unthankful, unholy, unloving, unforgiving, slanderers, without self-control, brutal, despisers of good, traitors, headstrong, haughty, lovers of pleasure rather than lovers of God, having a form of godliness but denying its power."* It will be difficult to find genuine faith on the earth when the Son of Man comes. (See Luke 18:8.)

Furthermore, the time is coming when the church will be taken out of the world, and then an awful state of things will go on in this earth, as described in the book of Revelation.

Again, there can be no question in the mind of anyone today that there has been a terrible moral decline in the past few years. This may be seen in the business world. Many of the leading businessmen, whom everyone has trusted, have been found guilty of a misapplication of funds that is so great it should have landed them in the penitentiary. This may also be seen in the terrible increase in immorality in all classes of society. Shameless adultery is on the increase. Divorces are multiplying; men are divorcing their wives and marrying other women with apparently no sense of shame. The increase of immorality among young men and women is appalling. Suicide is becoming alarmingly common. All this is undoubtedly due to the spread of skeptical and unbelieving views. Belief in a horrible future hell has declined enormously in the past few years.

Even many ministers of the Gospel neither preach nor believe in a dreadful hell. Everywhere, people are questioning the authority and inerrancy of the Bible—in universities and theological seminaries and in supposedly orthodox pulpits. This appalling harvest of evil and sin is simply the result of the sowing of the seeds of skepticism and unbelief.

INDEX

God (*continued*)
    and judgment, 123–24
    names of, 91–92
    nature of, 96–102
    and prayer (*see* prayer)
    and predestination, 146–48
    and prosperity, of wicked,
      148–49
    and punishment, of wicked
      (*see* afterlife; annihila-
      tion, of wicked; eternal
      punishment; hell; im-
      mortality; judgment;
      predestination; salva-
      tion, after death)
    and trouble, 172–73
    trust in, 121–22 (*see also*
      faith)
    wisdom of, 26, 28, 78, 103–
      04, 135, 148
    See also Holy Spirit; Jesus
      Christ
good works
    credited to us, 79
    importance of, 34–35
    meriting heaven by, 104–05
    rewards for, 153
grace
    falling from, 83–84 (*see
      also* unpardonable sin)
    growth in (*see* sanctifica-
      tion)
    versus works, 104–05
guardian angels, 106
guilt
    for original sin, 134–35
    salvation from, 19, 158, 178
      (*see also* Atonement)
heathen, 107–09
heaven, 109–13
    Bible as guide to, 80–82,
      111, 117–18

heaven (*continued*)
    good works as way to merit,
      104–05
    happiness in, 112–13
    how to be accepted into,
      104–05, 110–11 (*see also*
      backsliding; Christian
      life)
    as a place or state, 109–10
    recognition of loved ones in,
      111–12
    when our spirits go to, 11
hell, 112–13, 113–14
    See also Devil; eternal
      punishment
Holy Spirit, 114–16
    baptism with, 34, 115–16,
      143
    convicts of sin, 58–59
    dwells within believers,
      114–15, 179
    illuminates conscience, 55–
      56
    inspired Bible, 25–30
    prayer to, 142–43
    sin against (unpardonable
      sin), 173–77 (*see also*
      falling from grace)
    as third person of Trinity,
      101–02
    See also God; Jesus Christ
immortality, 117–19
    See also afterlife
Incarnation, 15, 19–20, 37–38,
    59–60
infants, salvation of, 119–21
Ingersoll, Robert Green, 60
inspiration, of Bible, 25–30
insurance, and trust in God,
    121–22